Out-Executing the Competition

Out-Executing the Competition

Building and Growing a Financial Services Company in Any Economy

Irv Rothman

WILEY

John Wiley & Sons, Inc.

Published by John Wiley & Sons, Inc., Hoboken, New Jersey.
Published simultaneously in Canada.

For general information on our other products and services or for technical support, please contact our Customer Care Department within the United States at (800) 762-2974, outside the United States at (317) 572-3993 or fax (317) 572-4002.

Wiley also publishes its books in a variety of electronic formats. Some content that appears in print may not be available in electronic books. For more information about Wiley products, visit our web site at www.wiley.com.

Library of Congress Cataloging-in-Publication Data
Rothman, Irv.
    Out-executing the competition : building and growing a financial services company in any economy / Irv Rothman. – 1
        p. cm.
    Includes index.
ISBN 978-1-118-31261-2 (cloth); ISBN 978-1-118-40903-9 (ebk);
ISBN 978-1-118-40904-6 (ebk); ISBN 978-1-118-40905-3 (ebk)
    1. Rothman, Irv.   2. Investment advisors–United States–
Biography.   3. Stockbrokers–United States–Biography.   4. Finance–United States.   5. Investments–United States.   I. Title.
    HG4928.5.R685A3 2012
    332.1092–dc23
    [B]
                                        2012014507

Printed in the United States of America

10 9 8 7 6 5 4 3 2 1

Gutsball *Noun: The ability to overcome apprehension or anxiety and rise to the occasion. 2. To feel free to take action while acknowledging potential consequences, but not fearing them.*

Contents

Preface

I t's a question I hear all the time: How did you get here from there?

In my case, "here" is the chief executive's office of Hewlett-Packard Financial Services, where for the past ten years I've been in charge of HP's captive finance business. If it were a standalone entity, our company would rank among the Fortune 1,000. It's a multibillion-dollar global operation that employs about 1,500 people worldwide, some of them working from our Berkeley Heights, New Jersey, headquarters. We have offices in more than 50 countries.

And "there"? Somewhat humble beginnings in the blue-collar neighborhoods of Bayonne, New Jersey, just west of New York City across the Hudson River. I was educated at Bayonne High School and Rutgers University before enlisting in the Army Reserves. I cut my teeth with a Wall Street brokerage house and then moved on to the equipment leasing industry, which has commanded my time, attention, and professional commitment for almost four decades.

It is, of course, a gross understatement to say that the business world is a far different place today from what it was in 1970, at the beginning of my career. Still, the basic principles of effective leadership remain consistent and unchanging. You have to be aware of what's needed if you're going to be able to cope and succeed. You've got to be open and adaptable, exhibit a continual curiosity, and be a willing learner. You've got to be flexible and alert to a society that is indeed changing—more diverse, less tied to tradition, but indisputably more connected in every conceivable way.

There are constants as well, and they are at least equally important. You must build a foundational set of principles—clearly defined operating philosophies that are your anchors as you address the rapidly changing circumstances of your world. Others must know what to expect from you—how you react under pressure and what you stand for. You need those around you to have trust and confidence that you'll do the right thing, the first time and every time.

Sounds simple, right? It isn't. People are always trying to figure out the elements of success—what works, what doesn't, how you get through those personal and career battles that everyone has to fight. Executives have been known to succumb to ego and hubris. They can lose sight of their core values and forget what it was that made their leadership style successful. They can forfeit all or part of those essential characteristics that produced a unique and exciting vision.

Stories of how best to avoid pitfalls and keep your eye on the ball are never wasted reading. That's why, although it is not intended to be an autobiography, this book features personal and professional vignettes from my life that have made me who I am today. I'd venture to say that, for any well-rounded, achievement-driven executive, the personal is at least as important as the professional. Discipline, focus, and dedication derive as much from our personal pursuits as from our activities in the corner office.

Here's an example: During the past year, I added boxing to my workout routine. Twice a week now, I haul my butt out of bed at 5 A.M. and head to the gym. My trainer is there to greet me. I work on the speed bag and the heavy bag. I jump rope and do a few rounds in the ring, usually followed by a whole series of weird boxing fitness exercises. It is exhausting, exhilarating, expansive work—and somehow purifying. On days I'm not boxing, I'm lifting weights, also at an ungodly early hour and under the supervision of my long-time "tormentor," Ivona.

It was my wife, Fraenzi, who introduced me to the boxing world, exposing me to things I had never considered before, things I realize now that I can't live without (more on that later). That's another characteristic of the successful executive: a willingness to adapt and absorb, even as you head toward the latter part of your career.

These chapters are about a kind of evolution—my own and that of the world of corporate America. They are about dealing with the challenges of social and corporate change by consistently adhering to a set of ideals. The stories in this book are intended to offer useful information for those with all sorts of life and work aspirations. You might even chuckle at a story or two. Who knows?

By the time my grandchildren (Leo, Max, Ben, Julia, and Alex) are old enough to read and (I hope) appreciate this, maybe technology will have made it possible for them simply to absorb these ideas in a Vulcan mind meld sort of way (hats off to Trekkies everywhere). It's hard to imagine that there won't be some more sophisticated, faster way than reading to get information.

Over the course of my life, I've been blessed with family, friends, and colleagues who've helped me reach my personal and professional goals. Those in my personal life who've made that part of the journey so especially rewarding are Fraenzi, the "Brash Basher from Basel"—who has taught me from a multicultural perspective how to enjoy and appreciate life—and my children, Allison and Harlan.

In my career, I've been especially fortunate to work with a core group of consummate professionals for more than 25 years— Gerri Gold, Dan McCarthy, Tom Adams, Rich Olson—and I'm grateful to all of them for their dedication, counsel, and service as role models during our years together at AT&T Capital, Compaq Financial Services, and now HPFS. They've made me a better leader and person. We've also had quite a few laughs along the way. My assistant, Kathleen Smerko, has been invaluable on a daily basis and in preparation of this book. Lastly, I would like to acknowledge the contributions of Scott Ladd, without whom this effort could not have been completed.

Since I dictated the opening thoughts of this project into a small tape recorder, I've wondered frequently: What do I have to offer current and future generations of business professionals? How can recollections from my career, my own particular brand of leadership and strategic philosophy, enrich their professional growth and understanding? What can I tell them that will assist them as they build and manage successful businesses?

I'm not Jack Welch or Bill Gates. I'm certainly not world-famous or even particularly well known outside the finance and leasing industry. I've learned my share of important lessons, though, so think of this as one guy's reflections about how life choices and decisions—some of them unambiguous, others considerably less straightforward—took him eventually from Point A to Point Z.

Preface

I hope that these career lessons illustrate how a truly innovative, proactive business strategy, philosophy, and managerial approach are crafted, and how they lead to the achievement of objectives that, at the start, might seem distant and unattainable.

Irv Rothman
July 2012

Out-Executing the Competition

Chapter 1

Craziest Idea I've Ever Heard—Let's Do It!

As a boy growing up in New Jersey, I never envisioned a career in finance leadership. No, I wanted to be a sports journalist. In fact, I wanted to be the next Mel Allen, the baseball broadcasting legend. Allen was a guy from Birmingham, Alabama, who, arguably, was the preeminent baseball announcer in the country. He was the voice on the other side of the radio wires as I listened to my beloved New York Yankees during the 1950s and 1960s.

I watched them play on television as well, of course, but in those days, well before cable sportscasts, we could see only the Yankees' home games on Channel 11, WPIX, in New York. I'll never forget Allen's famous catchphrase—"Hello out there, ever'body!"—that began his broadcasts. Today, I often use this effusive greeting to open teleconference meetings.

I thought there was no better, more exciting way to make a living. My mother had other ideas: "That's no job for a nice Jewish boy." (Clearly, she had no clue about Mel Allen's religious background; he was another nice Jewish boy.) At the time, although it was certainly disappointing to hear those words, somehow I knew she was right. I wouldn't be the next Mel Allen.

Nevertheless, my career path has delivered me to the role I believe I was born to fulfill. I still love the Yankees, but that dream of being the voice and face of the Bronx Bombers is now a distant memory, however fond. My days as CFO of AT&T Capital Corp., then later as CEO of Compaq Financial Services—were in retrospect, natural progressions in a life I believe has been defined by a passionate, driven desire to succeed and leave my mark on the American corporate landscape.

Each executive's journey to the pinnacle of corporate leadership has its own stories, its lessons learned and ignored. Each journey is unique. Like fingerprints, no two are exactly alike. My own journey hasn't been without a few missteps along the way, a miscalculation or two. But it's a journey colored for the most part by an operating philosophy that has served not only me well, but has also served my companies and the people who have worked for me over the years.

Certainly, it's been put to the test. We've endured three debilitating recessions during my tenure, including our most recent economic meltdown, the likes of which I had never seen. However, we've survived these difficult times well, coming out in better shape than most businesses for more than a quarter century, spanning senior leadership roles at AT&T, Compaq, and, since 2002, Hewlett-Packard.

Success in business is born of equal parts hard work and simply out-hustling the other guy (getting your fingernails dirty, if you will); taking calculated risks and keeping an open mind to innovation, no matter how out there it seems; understanding the global economy and the markets that define your business growth and potential; and learning as thoroughly as you can the industry in which you operate.

Simply put, you can't steal second base by keeping your foot on first. I've had to fight through an entangling thicket of management risk at many points along my career path—taking 180-degree turns in the midst of billion-dollar projects, telling bosses things they didn't want to hear, seeking approval for initiatives that defied conventional wisdom.

Lessons from the executive office leave their mark for good or bad. They can be like shrapnel, inflicting damage that takes a period of healing to overcome. Sometimes these lessons serve to elevate you above the fray, above the myriad obstacles to the next phase of your particular journey.

★　　★　　★

How do you develop and master a business philosophy that will guide you the length of a career that's a high-wire negotiation with no safety net below? Sometimes, it begins with a grilled-cheese sandwich.

It was the mid-1980s, less than a year after I had joined what would eventually become AT&T Capital. It was a time of economic volatility, marked by lots of merger mania and a national economy rebounding after years of inertia. American corporations hungered for expansion and increased revenue, wanting to grow new and innovative businesses.

AT&T Capital—originally AT&T Credit Corp.—was the financing and leasing arm of AT&T. At the time, I was serving as

CFO, the number two in a business that was picking up steam but having to make tough choices regarding its operational direction. We had an opportunity to develop a financing model for small telephone systems, one that could be perfect for small business customers. I understood early on that such an enterprise in the United States might involve hundreds, maybe more than a thousand, deals a day.

No doubt, it would be hugely labor-intensive, requiring countless schedules and innumerable company staff. In other words, a massive amount of data would have to be managed every day. Even more challenging, it required a full-out corporate commitment if we were to have any chance of success.

Still, the concept was untested. AT&T was more than a little reluctant to commit the funding we needed to build a back office for this project. At least internally. Eventually they warmed to the idea, however, on the condition that we lay off operations responsibility (read: the risk of investing budget dollars in such an opportunity) to somebody else. The potential of this thing was enormous—hundreds of millions, if not billions, of dollars. So we outsourced it to Chase Manhattan Bank, a classically organized command-and-control operation.

Normally, that would have given us supreme confidence; however, it soon became quite apparent that Chase was screwing it up. In retrospect and understandably, AT&T didn't care who was responsible for screwing it up. Poor execution was costing them substantial revenues, and we were the face of a project that was making many of my colleagues very nervous.

This was more than a situation where a company might pull the plug on an inefficient or money-losing department. The concept of a captive finance company within the AT&T empire was a notion that held extraordinary promise, and here it was, veering toward the ditch. None of us wanted to see it that happen, but what could be done to ensure that this promising idea would remain on track?

In early 1986, President and COO Tom Wajnert called me into his office and laid it on the line. "I want you to take oversight responsibility," he said. One could take the view that he wanted to distance himself from what appeared to be an impending disaster. The two people running the operation for us at the time, Gerri Gold and Jim Tenner, were high performers trying to fix a huge mess, and I feared they were about to watch their extremely promising careers circle the drain before they'd even had a chance to succeed.

Gerri was bright, energetic, and highly motivated. She had joined us after earning a degree in business administration from the University of Michigan and an MBA from New York University. Jim was a product of Middlebury College in Vermont and held a Masters from Dartmouth's Tuck School of Business. They had worked under AT&T Treasurer, S. Lawrence "Larry" Prendergast as part of the original study team that wrote the business plan for the captive finance business.

They were intelligent and already accomplished, with big futures if they could make this project work. We were struggling to devise an operating methodology that could turn this lemon into lemonade when Gerri and Jim approached me one day and suggested we meet with one of the consultants advising American Transtech. Transtech, a sister subsidiary company at AT&T, was a securities process business—in effect, a processing clearinghouse—that had a unique approach to organizational design.

Its idea was to organize small, autonomous teams of employees with broad responsibility to operate without the stricture of a linear management style. Although common to many American businesses these days, it was a radical concept in the 1980s. In practice, it created a laissez-faire work environment. Transtech personnel often came to work (well before the dot-com era, when such workplace uniforms became routine) in shorts and T-shirts with their hair in ponytails—and I am referring to the guys!

This unorthodox structure was the brainchild of Transtech consultant Paul Gustavson. Gerri and Jim arranged for all of us to get together for lunch and talk about Gustavson's approach to running a business. Lunch? I never do lunch, unless it's with customers. Otherwise, it's a complete waste of time. Still, I agreed to the meeting. Gerri and Jim had been persuasive. They were true believers that this concept would work.

Gustavson was a graduate of Brigham Young University with a Masters in organizational behavior. We couldn't have been more different. I was a kid from New Jersey with a penchant for throwing elbows in a very competitive East Coast business environment; he was a Mormon and a veteran of religious missions to Africa on behalf of his church. The personal differences didn't end there. I was a former basketball player; he was a walk-on who played for the well-regarded football coach Lavell Edwards at BYU in the early 1970s.

I later learned that Gustavson's fascination with leadership and strategy, and the impact they have on performance, derived from his days on and off the football field with Edwards. Most creative business strategists who make the kind of lasting impact that Gustavson did can cite that kind of relationship somewhere along their career development path, with a mentor or boss whose lessons stick with you and guide your own professional growth.

Gustavson had started his own consulting firm, Organization Planning and Design, Inc., in 1984. In the ensuing years, he's consulted with a veritable *Who's Who* of major U.S. corporations. His expertise in the area of business strategy, organizational design, knowledge management, team development, and change management is unchallenged. Today, I'd describe him as a true workplace visionary.

But I certainly wasn't prepared to concede that point as we arrived for lunch at a crummy diner in Paramus, New Jersey. There I sat with my two young stalwarts, leaning over that grilled cheese sandwich and a diet Coke and wondering what the hell I was doing there. For 90 minutes, Gustavson described in detail his vision of the socio-technical organization. That's what he called it, Socio-Tech, and it was quite a departure. He went on about how it was a "customer-in" approach, minimizing handoffs, controlling variances at the source, and linking key systems. These included information systems, targeted incentive compensation, new measurements of performance, even the office seating chart. Most importantly, it was about driving the behaviors and feelings among the employees so that they would and could better serve the customer and produce optimal results. His model looked like Figure 1.1.

The essence of his message was this: Organizations are perfectly designed to get the results they get. In other words, you get

ALIGNMENT

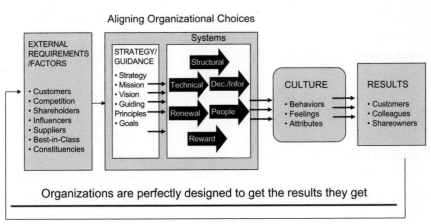

Figure 1.1   Aligning Organizational Choices

what you design for, whether that be a positive or negative outcome. Organize people in teams, equip them with the right tools, and they will manage themselves, he said. Employees would need to be cross-trained so that if credit and collections were off one month, you could ship everybody over there. If contracts and bookings were low, you would move employees to that group.

People cross-trained and multi-disciplined, organized to be ultra responsive and with those closest to the customer actually making daily decisions—what a concept! I'd long held the belief that people want to come to work every day and do a good job. Forget hierarchy. That was the kind of model I had witnessed at Chase, and look what a disaster hierarchical management there had turned out to be. Their command-and-control approach to management didn't reflect the needs of the marketplace. It had to go. Not just at Chase, of course, but across U.S. companies at the highest leadership levels.

We couldn't continue with the standard business philosophy of senior executives sitting in a conference room, dictating policy. Yet when we started out on our mission to remake the work experience more than 25 years ago, command and control was as embedded in our business culture and psyche as any system. To me, command and control was a rigidly top-down model. Rather than lifting employees to their highest potential in an environment that offered exciting work for maximum compensation based on merit, the system instilled fear and forced fealty from employees.

For years now, that's been the common and correct perception, I believe, about the value of such a management style. There have been no shortages of academic and organizational studies over the years that have more or less reinforced the notion that it does not work. A few years ago, Harvard Business School surveyed more than a million employees, most of them employed by Fortune 500 companies, about a wide range of workplace experiences and issues.

What did they like and not like about their jobs? How were they treated by managers? If they had been there for a long time, did they still maintain their initial energy and interest in the job? What was morale like throughout the organization? The Harvard researchers reached one key conclusion—in order to be successful, management had to stop demotivating workers, because motivation was dangerously low in too many places.

Employees are usually quite enthusiastic when they begin a new job. The Harvard study found, however, that in about 85 percent of companies, morale tends to drop like a stone in a pond after only six months, sinking steadily deeper with the passage of time until production is at minimum.

The solution? Here are a few that leap out:

- Instill an inspiring purpose.
- Recognize the high achievers in ways that tend to raise their game even more.
- Expedite career growth and company contribution.
- Provide proper, effective training.
- Communicate fully.
- Promote teamwork.
- Listen to what your employees have to say.

Beware of the conventional command-and-control structure. It can become a de facto killer of morale, enthusiasm, and, ultimately, productivity.

The concept of making our company more inclusive for all our people—even democratic, in a manner of speaking—was paramount as we pieced together our operating model. As we pushed forward in those foundational AT&T Credit days, we figured that groups should be designed by a cross-section of personnel across the business. Sales employees, the IT department, contracts administration, the financial group—the broadest possible mix of the AT&T Credit team—needed to be involved.

★　　★　　★

Today, those assumptions have been more than fully affirmed. But that day in Paramus, I wondered whether the Gustavson model was too simplistic. I listened intently to him talking passionately about all of this. I don't think Gerri and Jim breathed the entire hour and a half. I was 38 years old at that point, and I'd already had leadership responsibilities for quite some time. I thought I knew a little something about how to run a business.

"This guy's a bleeping communist," I thought. (Never a compliment under the best of circumstances, and this was a year before President Reagan issued his "tear down this wall" ultimatum to Mr. Gorbachev.) But Gustavson began striking a responsive chord as I reflected on the maddening inefficiency of the current Chase approach—27 handoffs, pieces of paper floating to the floor, critical tasks undone, customers neglected. We needed to streamline that to far fewer steps, a more reasonably managed number of tasks, better customer service. Here was Gustavson, writing a blueprint for me to do that. What he was talking about was suddenly so clear it was as though a light bulb was going on above my head.

Employees having ownership of the business is an important concept. When companies grow, they inevitably get bigger, more complicated, and maybe unwieldy. People can feel lost and directionless, unmotivated. Business history books are littered with stories of damaged morale and enterprise failure. You need to figure out how to keep a big company small. All the people who work for you, from the most junior salesperson to the senior vice president, must enjoy an environment in which they come to work every day feeling a genuine sense of ownership of the business, by recognizing their contribution to its success. That's hardly possible in large bureaucracies.

By the time we'd paid the bill and were walking out the diner door, I knew this was the way to go. If we adopted this style, our employees would have that sense of ownership of the business; they would understand its principles.

"This is the craziest idea I've ever heard," I told my team. "Let's do it."

Like most out-of-the-box thinking, it was followed by mixed results as we installed the new, innovative, and potentially risky operating plan. Some months we did well; some months we experienced challenges. Every time we had a bad month and things didn't go swimmingly, everybody else at the AT&T Credit senior leadership level was ready to trash the experiment.

I was fiercely protective, however, of the idea and of my team. I used to virtually put Gerri and Jim behind me and say, "You can't touch them. Over time, this is going to work; we just have to iron out the kinks." There were lots of knockdown, drag-out battles around our conference table and with the people cutting the checks at AT&T headquarters. But in the end, we prevailed. Our plan was vindicated. Eventually, that mess turned into a business with a 35 percent return on investment.

Today, that operating philosophy continues to guide the way we manage our company and interact with our customers. We've installed it along the way at Compaq Financial Services, and you can see it to this day in the management of Hewlett-Packard Financial Services.

Its key operating principles are built around having the employees own the business, with those closest to the customer making decisions. Autonomy, measurement aligned with business objectives, compensation—each of these is a vital element in putting this principle into practice. Sharing the wealth with those who create it is a highly motivational approach.

Word of our practices filtered through the financial services community. We began to see recognition for the model we'd developed based on Gustavson's concepts. A few years later, *New York Times* reporter Claudia Deutsch stopped by to profile our operation for an article on how to build a winning workplace environment. We spent time with her explaining in detail how we'd come up with this idea, how it was implemented, and why it was so successful.

Even in 1991, five years after my propitious meeting with Gustavson, the concept hadn't yet taken root across the American business landscape. At one point, Ms. Deutsch asked me: "Doesn't it make you nervous, delegating so much of the work to others?" A fair question, I thought, but the answer was easy. How many tens of thousands of customers do we have? I couldn't make every single decision.

Leadership is about finding a plan you're confident will work—even if it's fraught with risk, even if it scares your corporate bosses to death. It's about building and entrusting a management team that shares your vision, then letting them develop teams of dedicated people to embrace these business principles and make them their own.

Perhaps above all, it's about trusting your own instincts to set an operation into motion. Has that always worked for me? More times than not it has, though there are a few cautionary notes in my personal diary. Does it make you nervous, wondered the *Times* writer during our interview? Not if the risk is built on a foundation of good, reasoned, business calculation, a strategy that makes basic sense, and reliance on the right people with similar strategic thinking to execute it.

Those leadership faculties accrue over the years. If you're fortunate, they steer you toward becoming the CEO of a company you love, where you are responsible for the productivity and well-being of a large and dedicated group of employees. For me, this work in progress was born of a childhood on the banks of the Hudson River.

Chapter 2

Proud Son of Bayonne

I'm a Hudson County, New Jersey kid, 100 percent. To me, that means scrappy, industrious, and hard working. I was typical of the kids born and raised in the shadows of Manhattan in the 1940s, 1950s, and 1960s. Jersey City was my birthplace, but Bayonne was where I spent most of my youth and certainly where I collected most of my formative experiences.

Bayonne was like many other New Jersey cities in the middle of the last century—blue-collar, a mix of Italian, Irish, Germans, and Poles—Jews and Catholics alike. It's been said that the name Bayonne came from the city of the same name in France in which the Huguenots settled for a year or so in the seventeenth century before the founding of New Amsterdam. Is the story real or apoc-ryphal? No one seems to know for sure, but it was hardly Darien, Connecticut, or Beverly Hills, California. Johnny Carson used to poke fun at his bandleader Doc Severinsen's outfits by noting that his tailor was "Raoul of Bayonne."

What I do know is that Bayonne was home for my family and me. My dad was in retail, working in the liquor business. He had served a three-year-plus tour of duty in Europe during World War II, and he had a certain worldliness about him that I admired. Like many men of his generation, however, he spent long and odd hours at work to keep food on the table. We'd share Sundays as a family, but otherwise I didn't see him all that much. We did have one routine that was kind of special: going to the bakery for bagels and to the appetizing store for lox, picking up a Sunday *New York Times*, and coming home to sit around the table for an extended breakfast.

When the weather cooperated, we'd "have a catch" on Sundays —to some, that will be known as playing catch. Of course, my father was exhausted, half dead, his only day off of the week. We'd toss the baseball for 15 minutes or so, then he'd say, "Time!" It never seemed enough, but I was always grateful for even that much. Do I wish my father had done more with me, had been able to devote more time? He was working hard, doing the best he could.

When I got to be 9 or 10, sometimes I'd get to stay up late on Saturday nights until Dad came home. It might be 10:30, but he often showed up with ice cream or a pizza. Small moments, but they mattered. He knew I'd be up watching *Gunsmoke* or some other favorite show, and we'd catch up on the day, maybe talk about how the Yankees were doing.

In retail, the weeks between Thanksgiving and Christmas were crazy, and we rarely saw him. My birthday falls between these two holidays, so it was doubly hard. He even used to have to go in to work on Sundays. When I got older, I'd accompany him and help out. We never really bothered with Chanukah. Hudson County was and probably still is the most intensely Catholic county on the eastern seaboard. To give you an idea of the Catholic influence, a higher percentage in Hudson County voted for John F. Kennedy for president in 1960 than in any county in his home state of Massachusetts. So on Christmas morning, when Dad was finally able to be home, we usually celebrated an observance of "something."

★   ★   ★

A chain smoker, my dad died at the age of 53. His father before him, also a smoker, had died young as well. A smoker myself, I realized I had to quit or invite the same fate. In 1971, I lit my last cigarette and haven't smoked since.

My father's death hit me hard. About a month later, I came across an article in the *Sunday New York Times Magazine* about healthy lifestyles and how aerobics exercise can make a difference. I had already resolved not to follow my father to an early grave. I would take matters into my own hands and defy the Rothman Curse. I would live a long, healthy, and productive life.

For the past 35 years, my attention to physical health and well-being has been as important to me as everything that depends on it. I kept that resolution. I've been an avid workout guy, tennis player, and golfer most of my life, and my second wife, Fraenzi, introduced me to boxing two years ago.

Fraenzi's brother, Richard, is the business manager for the champion boxer, Oscar de la Hoya and CEO of Golden Boy Promotions. (Swiss banking used to be the family business, now it's boxing, go figure.) Boxing is an invigorating and satisfying pursuit. They don't call it the sweet science for nothing.

15

My father's bequests included another critical lesson—I was determined to make sure I spent quality time with my own children, having been denied that pleasure too often with my own father because of his health or, more frequently, his highly demanding work schedule. My paternal relationships would be different. And they were.

You can't always be there for family events if you're running a complex global business. The road will take you where it must, and my roles as CFO, division president, and more recently, CEO tended to throw up roadblocks. But I did my best, rarely missing my kids' games, school plays, or other important events. My daughter, Allison, did all the dance recitals, school plays, and, early on, soccer games. I fondly recall sharing the joy of those experiences with her. Photos simply can't capture the sheer happiness you see in a son or daughter's face while they're participating in one of their favorite activities.

I remember a business trip when my son, Harlan, was about three years old. One night, I called home from the road as usual. "When are you coming home, Daddy?"

I wasn't sure. "Looks like Friday night," I told him.

In an incredulous tone that I can still hear today, "You mean you're not going to be home for Halloween!?!" Halloween was Thursday. I assured him I'd figure out a way to get home on time, even if it meant cutting short my trip, and we managed to do a costumed tour of the neighborhood—Trick or Treat!

Years later, he was playing in the Little League championship game. I had a business dinner that night, something I probably should have been attending, but instead I sent my regrets. When the dinner organizer asked why, I explained, "If his team loses, he'll need somebody to console him, and if he wins, he'll want me to share it with him." I said I thought it was a no-brainer; I think the guy thought I was nuts. But it wasn't a negotiable point for me.

As a senior in high school, Harlan was captain of the soccer team. When we received the team's schedule during the summer, I immediately passed it along to my secretary to see how it stacked up against what we knew of my calendar at that moment. "Bad news," she said. "You can only make three games the whole season."

That wouldn't do. "Jean, start changing things, I'm going to try to get to all the home games and if I can get to some road games, better still." So schedules were changed. I've never doubted it was the right thing to do. I'd go to the games and head right back to the office. I've never believed there aren't enough hours in a day.

During my own early years, my dad just couldn't do that. It was my mother who filled that vacuum. She was the one who came to most of my Little League games, my violin recitals and concerts, my school plays. Mom did the parent-teacher conferences. Of course, it wasn't all that unusual in those days. Many fathers were missing in action when it came to raising their children or taking an active role in their lives. Dads worked, moms stayed at home and ran the house and raised the children—a different era.

My mother probably wasn't always thrilled to be there. Often, she would bring her knitting or the *New York Times* crossword puzzle, to games especially. But whenever I looked up into the stands, there she was.

Later, as much as business demands weighed on me 24/7, I accepted no substitute for sharing in those special moments. Your kids don't care that you worked until midnight closing a deal; they do care if they glance up into the stands and you're nowhere to be seen. Excuses are not the same as being there. My mom being an active participant in those aspects of my life was priceless.

★   ★   ★

My mother's parents were religious. We kept a kosher home, though I think my mother did it mostly to keep her parents off her back. On those rare occasions that we went out on Sunday mornings for breakfast, the menu often included bacon and eggs. My father's army experience taught him that you had to do what you had to do when it came to army rations. Not a lot of kosher meals in the field during wartime.

As for my own Jewish education, I was schooled at the local temple where I had a very good relationship with the cantor. He was bound and determined to make me into a cantor myself. My father thought that would have been the coolest thing since sliced bread. I greatly preferred being at basketball practice and made sure never to miss one; I can't say the same for those sessions with Cantor Lencz.

The traditions of the Jewish religion were important to me. I have two grown children now, with lives and families of their own. My daughter is extremely attached to the whole notion of the faith. My son couldn't care less. When you're a parent, you want to teach your kids, but when they're old enough, they'll make their own choices. My job was to ensure that my children's choices would be well informed.

Money was tight when I was growing up. We didn't take a family vacation until I was 13 years old, a driving trip to Canada. We spent a few days in and around Montreal. On the ride back, we headed back down through New England. We have family in Providence, and we had a great time seeing our Rhode Island cousins. They treated us like gold, even though we kids didn't know each other all that well. We had a terrific time. I still remember that trip.

We spent the first summers of my life in Long Beach, on Long Island just east of New York City. My grandparents had a house there. It was real 1950s stuff. Women went out for the summer with their kids, and the men came out on the weekends.

My mom had an adventurous streak. When I was 12, maybe 13, she often took me driving in the family car at daybreak in Long Beach—with one eye out for the cops at all times—to teach me how to drive years before I was eligible for a license. My mother, the renegade.

She also was the one who got me interested in basketball, the sport that would become my passion throughout high school. She had played basketball herself as a young girl and passed along that love of the game. My mom came from money, most of which my grandfather lost during the Depression. He had come to the United States years earlier on the boat from Austria by himself as a 13-year-old. In the 1930s, he was also instrumental financially in helping some of our relatives escape Nazi Europe for the safety of the United States. That had cost him what was left of his fortune after the economy had badly deteriorated.

I'm named for my paternal grandfather. My father's name was Herbert; my son Harlan is named for him. If you're Jewish, you're supposed to name your child after the closest family member who has died. About six weeks after my father died, we were having Sunday dinner at my in-laws' house. My first wife, Barbara, was pregnant with our second child, and we didn't know if the baby would be male or female.

My mother chimed in, "Of course if it's a boy, you are going to name him Herbert."

"If it's a boy, I'm not going to make the same decision you and Dad made to give him some awful name," I said. I got the short end of the stick on the naming rights; my brother is Jeffrey Mark. I'm Irving Harold.

Of my naming, my mother said, "Oh, that was your father's idea." My father was gone six weeks, and my mother didn't hesitate to throw him under the bus. That's my mother. I laughed my ass off.

What you're supposed to do is give the baby the Hebrew name. The Americanization of that tradition is to give him the exact name, or a name with the same first initial. They could have named me Isaac, Ian, or Ichabod, but they didn't. And they didn't even give me a middle name I could use. I decided to give my kids monosyllabic middle names, in case they wanted to use their first initial and their full middle names.

My personality today certainly is a distillation, to some degree, of the personalities of my parents, grandparents, and extended family. I think I've managed to take the best of what they taught me and make it part of my own philosophy, both personal and career-wise. My maternal grandfather came from Austria, my paternal grandfather from Russia. Both my grandmothers were born in New York City. My maternal grandmother had a sister, Aunt Jean, but it was my Uncle Lou, Jean's husband, who I enjoyed the most. As a little kid, I remember walking the beach with Lou, looking for change embedded in the sand. He'd point down and cry, "Look!" having dropped a nickel or a dime in the sand for me to find. I thought that was the coolest thing. Later, when I got to be a little older, Uncle Lou would take me with him to the racetrack. Lou loved the ponies, good cigars, and pinochle.

If my maternal grandfather, Julius, got mad at somebody, he'd say, "He should only drop dead in a corner," as if this was the most undignified place to expire. Julius had a dog, a Heinz 57 mutt, big and mean. Nobody could get near him, but he loved my grandfather—even though he used to yell at him, "In a corner!" as though cursing him to die in a corner. I never got to know my paternal grandfather, who died before I was born.

My maternal grandfather was a grumpy, cantankerous fellow. He used to say to me, "You're a grandson? What's so grand about you?" That was his sense of humor. "Oh, it's your birthday? I wasn't so happy you were born!" He really used to say stuff like that. Another of his sour expressions—"It's your America!"—has stayed with me all these years.

My mother's mother was tough as nails. She had four daughters and 10 grandkids. My personality, I think, is more like my mom's. She had a sense of humor; you could have some fun with her. That certainly wasn't the case with all of my relatives. As a girl, my mother took advantage of some of the amenities less fortunate girls didn't enjoy during her childhood. She went to sleep away camp, which was unusual in the 1930s. She had braces on her teeth, also a luxury at the time. Later, though she never graduated, she would spend time as a student at New York University.

$$\star \quad \star \quad \star$$

On my father's side of the family, there was only my grand-mother and my dad's younger brother Sanford, whom we all called Sandy and who was seven years younger than my dad. My dad never really moved back home after returning from the war, but Grandma Sarah and Uncle Sandy lived together—Sandy was a bachelor until well into his thirties—in a smallish apartment in Upper Manhattan. I'm sure it was economic circumstances that dictated this arrangement, but they were devoted to each other as well.

Given the lack of proximity and everybody's work schedule (Grandma Sarah worked retail as well, in a neighborhood dress shop), we didn't see them all that much, but when we did, it felt like a special occasion. My brother and I were the only grandchildren on that side and were accordingly doted on and spoiled.

I had a special relationship with my Uncle Sandy. I guess I was the little brother he never had. We went to Yankee Stadium in the spring, college football in the fall, and Madison Square Garden in the winter to watch the Knicks and NYU basketball. I hope he knew how much I appreciated all the time and attention.

Given the rare opportunity of a New York City sleepover, we'd go out and get the Sunday newspapers late on Saturday night, when the streets were teeming with people, with the rumble of the elevated subway overhead and me all wide-eyed, drinking it in. When Sandy finally married, he kept a longstanding promise —I was his best man, at 14 years old.

While basketball was my favorite sport growing up, I also played baseball throughout the early part of high school, in the local Babe Ruth League. Bayonne High School had close to 4,000 students at its peak, making it one of the largest public high schools in the state. Its athletic teams played at the Group 4 level, the most competitive state high school athletics division. Bayonne was exceptional in just about every sport. I really wanted to play on the baseball team, but the Bayonne team was too good. When they began throwing curveballs, it was time to take a seat on the sidelines.

I played basketball for the Bayonne Jewish Community Center team. This was no slouch team. We won the state championship. In my senior year, we made it all the way to the semifinals of a national tournament before losing by a single point. It was an exhilarating experience overall, even if it ended in bitter defeat. This was one of those moments when I realized that I hated to lose . . . at anything. All the Jewish "rejects" from the high school team played for the Community Center, and positions were highly competitive. There were a lot of good Jewish prospects in my city when I was growing up; several players on my team went on to play college ball.

Bill Broderick was the head coach of the Bayonne Jewish Community Center team. He had played college hoops and was a fabulous coach, well schooled in the Xs and Os and also a genuine motivator. As much as I respected and admired him, however, I thought he was a bit of a slave driver. It felt like we practiced seven days a week, 52 weeks a year. Insane. Weekends,

Thanksgiving, you name it. The only exception was Christmas morning. Obviously, basketball in Hudson County was very, very serious, almost a religion. It was all about hard work, discipline, and accountability.

Bill was a tremendous influence on me. He brought to his job a work ethic that made an indelible impression. I think those lessons remain with me to this day. They most certainly were important cogs in my development. Sure, he enjoyed winning, but it was far more than that. He emphasized teamwork and pulling together toward a common goal.

I absolutely loved basketball practice. It was almost a physical thrill to step on the court. There's really nothing quite like the smells and echoing sounds, the sweat and rawness of the activity itself. I eventually had the same feelings in playing golf and tennis. You just can't wait to get to the court or the course for something you relish doing. To be sure, that love of spending time in the gym was easily satisfied during my years playing for Bill.

One New Year's Eve, when I picked up my date, I was carrying a gym bag with my basketball stuff; I had just come from one of Bill's practices. Opening the door, her father asked, "What's in the bag?" I told him.

"He made you practice on New Year's Eve?" he asked incredulously.

"Not only that," I said, "we've got another one tomorrow morning."

That was my coach. No rest for the weary, not even on the holidays. We lived that aggressive, committed approach to basketball throughout our high school years. Our team was extremely competitive. We ran a sophisticated offense and defense. For example, we used a full-court zone press when hardly anyone in the country at the high school level knew what it was, then converted to man-to-man defense at half-court. Our opponents were confused throughout the whole game when they saw a different defensive set, four or five zones and man-to-man as well, every time they brought the ball up.

Bill, who was about 30 years old at the time and still a superb athlete, would participate in a practice occasionally. If he had the ball, and he drove by you while you were covering him, your ass was grass. "I'm over the hill, and I can still take you guys on!" he would bellow at us. Bill was an important early influence in my life. The lessons and virtues he imparted remain with me to this day. I'm certain that many of the characteristics that shape my business temperament and philosophy were created in the Petri dish that was the gymnasium of the Bayonne Jewish Community Center.

There were several mentors who served as personal role models in my early life, though the word "mentor" was never used in those times. But more than any person, it was a place—Camp Onibar—that made the most abiding impression on me during my teenage years. Tucked into the mountains of Wayne County in northeastern Pennsylvania, Onibar was a boys' camp with a sister facility, Camp Geneva, for girls.

I worked at Camp Onibar as a waiter and then as a waterfront counselor during the last three summers of high school and the first two summers of college. This camp was really my first exposure to a lifestyle I hadn't experienced. Rich families sent their children there. I didn't come from rich. It was eye opening.

Even now, I look back on those days and realize it was probably my favorite life experience. I looked forward to my summers there like nothing else. It was paradise: the mountains, the lake, spectacular scenery, clean air. The work was hard; waiting tables is no picnic. But the off hours were priceless, with time for basketball and swimming in the seemingly endless sunshine. My first summer there, I learned how to water ski. In 1962, that was a pretty glamorous sport for someone like me.

I really got to see how the other half lived. Most of the kids who spent their summers there were great. And it was just a pleasure to be around their parents, to see how they carried themselves, how they interacted. You can learn a lot just by observing.

Today, when you send your kids to sleep away camp, there are one or two days when the parents are permitted to be there.

In those days, things were different. Parents came and went as the spirit moved them. The camp maintained a guest lodge for visiting parents. They kept a separate dining area for parents, who could hang around by the lake, watch their kids take part in activities. For the campers, it might have been a little too much, an entire summer of Little League moms and dads. But as a counselor and observer, it was a remarkable learning experience for me.

Did it influence me to want to make money? Not per se, but it did present what the possibilities could be, showing me a style of life and living that was dramatically different from anything I had known.

Back in Bayonne, I was thinking about my future. I was a good enough student, I'd won a Scholastic Press Association of New Jersey award for sports writing as a senior, and I had been a decent athlete. I thought I'd have a lot to offer any college. I don't recall having any extended conversations with my parents about the vital issues of the day. When it came to my future, my career, where I might end up going to college, we didn't talk a lot about it.

It just wasn't like that in my house and, to be honest, I don't think it was very different for most of my friends. My parents weren't big on guidance. They were more critical than guiding, and it was hard to accept my father's criticism since he wasn't around that much.

I knew Mel Allen had nothing to worry about. My dreams of announcing the Yankees games were pretty much dashed after I heard from Mom. Even with the scholastic journalism award in my back pocket, my interests were already starting to move beyond broadcasting or sports journalism. I did know one thing. Rutgers University was not where I wanted to go to college. I had gotten a taste of life outside the urban landscape of northern New Jersey, and it was sweet.

Rutgers, our state university in New Jersey, was and is a fine school. It was affordable and that was probably the most important consideration for a family that wasn't wealthy. Back then, tuition was about $200 a semester with student fees adding another $60. If you lived on campus, the total cost was about $1,200 a year.

But that wasn't my vision, my adventure. There were maybe 770 kids in my high school graduating class, and 35 or 40 of the guys would be going to Rutgers, in New Brunswick. About an equal number of girls went off to Douglass, in those days the all-women's sister college that was part of the Rutgers system and just across town. Most of these were students I had known since the third grade. The same damn people. I desperately wanted to do something different. I wanted my college experience to be special.

I was interested in a small school in Pennsylvania, Muhlenberg College. Muhlenberg was everything I envisioned in a school. It was about as far from Bayonne and my life there as I could imagine. At urban Bayonne High, you had your greasers, your brains, and your jocks; the girls kind of moved among these groups. Well, maybe not so much the brains. We were an ethnically diverse city and school, tough and feisty. There were fistfights in the gym and all the other teenaged crap to be found in high school.

And then there was pastoral Muhlenberg, in the beautiful countryside, with ivy-covered walls, on a leafy campus. We didn't do a lot of leafy in Bayonne. Muhlenberg just seemed like nirvana to me. On top of that, the basketball coach was interested in me. Although Muhlenberg was a Division 3 school (no athletic scholarships), I wanted to play basketball there, and the coach knew Bill Broderick.

But the cost was a long way north of $1,200—maybe $5,000 a year after everything was considered. My parents and I took a drive out to the campus on Columbus Day in 1963. We had a meeting in the admissions office, which was wood-paneled and elegant. I met the basketball coach. We wandered around the campus, soaking it all in. As for actually matriculating at such a wondrous place, I might as well have hoped to be the first man on the moon. After we left the school, I remember the conversation with my dad as if it were yesterday. Calling it a conversation might be a bit of a stretch.

"You want to go to college, kid? Rutgers," he said. That was it. A pronouncement, not a discussion. So much for the gorgeous Muhlenberg campus. Leafy was not to be in my future.

Chapter 3

School Days, School Days . . .

S o off to Rutgers I went. The university was in New Brunswick, just down the New Jersey Turnpike about 35 minutes from home. The campus was pretty and accommodating in its own way; maybe not as green and lush as I wanted, but it would have to do.

I entered Rutgers against a backdrop of rising national campus protests opposing the war in Vietnam. Nowhere on the East Coast, except perhaps on the grounds of Columbia University in New York City, was the antiwar animus as pronounced and energized as it was at Rutgers. It was a time of student demonstrations and campus teach-ins organized to alert the masses to the evils of American aggression in Southeast Asia.

History was the major I chose. Rutgers had one of the most accomplished and respected history departments in the country—and notorious, as it would turn out to be while I was there. Early in the academic term of 1965–1966, my sophomore year, one of Rutgers' younger and most provocative history professors, Eugene Genovese, stood up at one of the campus teach-ins and announced himself a Marxist and a socialist, adding: "I do not fear or regret the impending Viet Cong victory in Vietnam. I welcome it."

Well, not surprisingly, Prof. Genovese's declaration of support for our nation's enemy created a firestorm. It came smack in the middle of the race for New Jersey governor that autumn of 1965, with politicians calling for his immediate ouster. National political figures the likes of Richard Nixon and President Lyndon B. Johnson joined the fray. Rutgers became a lightning rod in the growing debate over the U.S. course in Vietnam. *Time* magazine, in an extensive examination of the Rutgers political drama, described my university as "Berkeley of the East," referring to the West Coast center of student antiwar activism.

The Republican gubernatorial candidate, State Senator Wayne Dumont, demanded Genovese's head on a platter. Compelled to meet the swirling wave of controversy head on, Governor Richard Hughes, a Democrat seeking reelection, asked the Rutgers Board of Governors to conduct a thorough investigation of the 35-year-old Genovese and his public statements. The board would eventually respond with a vindication on the grounds that his dismissal would have violated his right of free speech.

Hughes won reelection, Genovese kept his job, and the flames of student antiwar sentiment, burned ever brighter not only on the college streets of New Brunswick but at universities across the country, eventually bringing down a presidential administration and laying the groundwork for an end to hostilities in the 1970s.

Genovese left Rutgers for positions at the University of Rochester, among other places, but this avowed Marxist never changed his stripes. He eventually co-created *Marxist Perspectives*, a journal dedicated to marketing socialist ideas across the United States. His co-creator? Warren Sussman, another renowned Rutgers history professor. Sussman exercised a major academic influence on my college development, even if his radical political views never appealed to my own more conservative philosophy. Like so many other students, I marveled at Sussman's knowledge and oratorical skill.

This was very early in the Vietnam conflict. I wasn't among the students chanting antiwar slogans in the square. This was not my thing. I was a financially struggling kid from Bayonne, primarily interested in my schoolwork, maintaining a strong academic record and earning enough money to keep going. Intellectually, I found the whole antiwar exercise fascinating, of course. This was a time of unprecedented activism on college campuses across America, the rise of the ever more radical student left.

The history department at Rutgers supported the rights of our professors to speak their minds and express their opinions on the war publicly. Sure, Sussman was left leaning politically, but he was very serious when it came to history. He was much respected in the academic world. Years later, when I was at AT&T, I attended a two-week seminar at Dartmouth College, a special leadership program that attracted leading figures from a broad variety of big companies.

During one of the sessions, one of the history professors from the Dartmouth faculty addressed us, a group of about 40. She didn't stand still behind the podium; instead, she took her shoes off and walked the room, comfortable in her presentation, with a focused grasp of her material. She was one of the revered professors at Dartmouth, and I was quite impressed by the lecture.

Later, we attended a closing cocktail party, most of the professors we'd met over the two weeks attended as well. I pulled the history professor aside and said, "You know, I've got to tell you something. I really enjoyed your lectures. Your presentation was fantastic. I was a history major at Rutgers, and I had a history professor there that you remind me of so much."

"His name is Warren Sussman," I said. She dropped her cocktail glass.

"I remind you of Warren Sussman? He's my idol!" she replied. She carried on for some time about what Sussman's writings and lectures had meant to her in the development of her own career in academia.

Sussman was like many in the history department, a remarkable intellect, thoroughly immersed in his subject, articulate, and engaging. People flocked to hear Sussman whenever he lectured. We had another professor, Peter Karanas, whose specialty was the Byzantine era. When Karanas lectured, you couldn't get a seat in the auditorium, especially when the subject was Empress Theodora, the sixth century empress whose life was randy and controversial.

She was thought to have spent time in her youth in a brothel, and Karanas, all 5′5″ tall with a shock of white hair, would prance about during his lectures imitating the empress in a manner that was at least mildly pornographic. Students rolled in the aisles during his Theodora lectures.

A. Carter Jefferson was another influential instructor who was also quite a character. He chain-smoked Eriks (those awful black mini cigars) during class while we listened to him speak eloquently in a pronounced Texas drawl of the French Revolution and the Napoleonic Era. I used to sit next to Jim Valvano in class, one of the stars of our basketball team and a future Hall of Fame college basketball coach. It was heady stuff.

I loved studying history. I was fascinated with the cast of professorial characters, the passion they brought to their subject matter, the intellectual rigor they embodied. I always imagined that none of them would want to do anything else for a living. There was something appealing to me about that notion—doing what you love and throwing every bit of your heart and soul into it. That was a lesson I took to heart; my history classes truly taught me more than the French Revolution and the Byzantine era.

★   ★   ★

I joined a fraternity at Rutgers—Sigma Alpha Mu, better known as "Sammy." There were 30 or so guys in my pledge class, and I was one of only 5 or 6 selected to live in the fraternity house after we were finally initiated. It seemed a big honor at the time.

I was assigned to arguably the nicest room in the house. When my folks came to visit during Parents Weekend that year, I gave them a tour and proudly showed off my room. My dad did a quick stroll and then declared, "This place is some fire trap." He was prescient; a year after I graduated, the place burned to the ground.

Financial support from the home front was in short supply, so, in order to make ends meet, I held four different jobs during my Rutgers years, pretty much simultaneously. One was serving as steward at Sammy, a position that involved planning breakfast, lunch, and dinner for our fraternity brothers, ordering the food, unloading the delivery trucks, paying the bills, and working alongside the cook to get the meals prepared and served. In exchange, I received free room and board, which was more than welcome.

There was a lot to like about my college fraternity experience. Sigma Alpha Mu was a predominantly Jewish fraternity. Our house was located just next door to Zeta Beta Tau, or ZBT, known also as "Zionist Bankers Trust" and "Zillions, Billions, and

Trillions." Sammys generally weren't as rich as Zeebs, but many of us were wealthy. I didn't have a car, but I had fraternity brothers who drove Corvettes and MGBs.

On Friday nights, we had Candlelight Night get-togethers. You could bring a date, and the menu was steak and lobster. Unfortunately, as I was working those dinners, I rarely had an opportunity to participate on a purely social level. I appreciate my college experience in many ways, but sacrifices had to be made. I didn't get to a Rutgers football game after my freshman year. Too busy.

My first year in the Sammy House, I shared a room with two other guys, a sophomore from my pledge class and a junior. The junior and I just never clicked. Part of my job was to fill in if one of the regular waiters didn't show, so I was waiting tables at the house one night. It was fish night, never a particularly popular meal, but as mother always emphasized, a balanced diet was important, so fish it was. Regardless of the meal, every dinner was jacket and tie in those days. Even if a guy wore the same jacket every night for four years, he couldn't be seated without it.

My junior roommate is busting my chops about how crappy everything is on this particular fish night. The food is lousy, the service is worse. I'm taking it and taking it. As I'm serving dessert—chocolate pudding—he makes some crack about me taking kickbacks from suppliers. That was just too much. I pushed the chocolate pudding into his face—kind of like James Cagney shoving that grapefruit into his girlfriend's face in *Public Enemy.*

I was furious. Everyone else thought it was funny. Naturally, a food fight ensued, fish and side dishes and pudding flying all over the dining room until dinner jackets were covered in food. I was fined 25 bucks for that little fracas. I couldn't afford 25 bucks. But stuff got broken and had to be cleaned up. To maintain some semblance of harmony in our room, I had taken so much crap for so long from this particular fraternity brother. I was getting room and board free and that was great. But the work was hard and thankless. And he impugns my integrity? Finally, I just couldn't contain myself. So I paid the fine, tough as it was.

Challenging my integrity . . . that wasn't kidding, that went beyond teasing. We didn't speak for the rest of the school year while we lived in the same room. It was interesting. I haven't had that kind of confrontation in my entire career, when someone questioned my motives or integrity. You're not going to see pudding flying around even the most contentious board room, I think it's safe to say. But I've always believed that I should be judged and should rise or fall on my own merits. I've never felt otherwise, and I've never wanted our employees to feel otherwise. This is what I've done; evaluate me on the result.

My other college jobs, thankfully, were less messy. In New Jersey back then, you could do substitute teaching if you had accumulated 60 undergraduate credits. During my junior and senior years, I kept Wednesdays and Fridays free from academic requirements to earn the additional pay of a substitute teacher.

I was teaching mostly in Jersey City. Jersey City is a city that has deservedly earned a reputation over the years as a tough, unyielding place. It was a very rough school district even then. I never taught a grade higher than fourth. No way I was going to teach kids older than 11. I was 142 pounds, soaking wet. Even some of those fourth-graders had size on me.

My life was in constant motion. I'd become so busy that friends I hadn't seen for a while would ask me if I had been sick, because I looked so skinny and had been out of touch for so long. For many of my fellow students, college was attending classes, studying, and socializing, with few other demands on their time. That was never an option for me.

I also had a territory on campus working for L.G. Balfour, the company that sells class rings, party favors, and similar merchandise. L.G. Balfour was based in Massachusetts, and they were setting up businesses on campuses across the country. I was one of four on-campus representatives at Rutgers. I used to operate a stand in the Rutgers Student Center, more commonly known as "The Ledge," on Tuesday nights from January to May, and worked my group of fraternities for the prizes they gave away on special weekends in the Rutgers social calendar.

Maybe the most instructive job I held during college, and the one most instrumental in preparing me for the working world I would eventually inhabit, was at Charles' Men's Wear in Jersey City. To say I learned from this experience about how business operates would be an understatement.

One expression I always favored and still use today—that "you can't sell from an empty wagon"—I picked up during my sales days at Charles'. It originated during the Depression, when people had to sell from carts on the street just to survive. It's a way of saying you have to have enough product, it has to be good, and it has to appeal to the broadest potential number of customers.

Charles Fiur, the man behind the name and my boss at the men's store, was an enormously successful guy. He had succeeded in business without benefit of much formal education. This wasn't a Brooks Brothers outlet, mind you. It was a medium-range men's retail store and very competitive in its market.

That sense of competition, however, wasn't limited to store against store. No, it was instilled and promoted equally within his own sales staff. Charles introduced an incentive compensation system for us. No customer ever walked out the door without talking to at least two salespersons.

Here I was, a college kid trying to learn the ropes in retail sales, a reasonably personable guy. But I couldn't always seal the deal with a customer. Who could? Sometimes, you need to bring in a closer. We had a series of verbal cues that we used. If a sale seemed to be slipping away, I would signal another salesman to come over and try to salvage it. Then I would step aside and the other salesman would give it a shot. The system also worked in reverse, with me as the closer from time to time.

We were nothing if not persistent. It was teamwork in its purest fashion. Yet it was highly competitive internally. Ultimately, you wanted to make the sale for the benefit of Charles and the store. But you also were determined to close it for yourself, to figure out the ways to be recognized for cunning and superior effort, not to mention making some extra money. I think that lesson—walking the fine line between full collaboration and yet trying to distinguish yourself enough through your own skills and strategy to catch the boss's eye—is something still with me to this day.

Looking back, I know that those experiences—basketball, camp, fraternity steward, and selling for Charles'—were essential building blocks in my career development. They taught me responsibility and accountability, the need to be industrious and to stay on task until the very end, even if at times it seemed an almost unattainable goal, and the importance of balancing individual achievement and excellence as a team player.

★   ★   ★

I had majored in history with plans to go to law school. The Vietnam War changed my mind. I was accepted at several law schools as I was leaving Rutgers, but at that time, there were no draft deferrals for law school.

Concurrently, I had applied for enlistment in the Army Reserves and was accepted into a reserve unit in December 1968. I was placed on active duty the following October. I served my six months' stint at Fort Jackson, South Carolina. My service time was relatively uneventful, thank goodness, but serving as a squad leader gave me the chance to continue building and refining my leadership capabilities.

Still, it was a strange time. As some soldiers were preparing for life and death in Vietnam, most of us reservists weren't thinking that way. Our attitude was, "Let's get through this the best way we can and then get on with our lives." My drill sergeant would say to me, "Rotham!" (He always mangled the pronunciation of my name in his southern drawl). "Rotham, I know we wearin' the same uniform, but we ain't in the same Army!" It was true. The Vietnam era was a time of class distinction in America, to put it mildly.

It's no secret that this was one of the most volatile periods in the history of our country. No American war in the twentieth century had generated such white-hot controversy. The war changed the political landscape, altering forever the course of events in the United States: Nixon's election in 1968, scandal and resignation in 1974, oil embargoes and gas lines, Carter's election and national malaise, and the election of Ronald Reagan, facilitated by a pervasive national anxiety and a hostage crisis in Iran that seemed to characterize the United States as powerless— susceptible to the whims of religious fanatics and helpless to implement a rescue.

My discharge from the Reserves came in March 1970. I returned to New Jersey, eager to get my life and career moving in the right direction. Though I had walked through the doors of Rutgers years earlier with thoughts of practicing law, it was now the business world I wanted to explore. I had gone from the college campus to Fort Jackson and felt the need to live a little less prescriptively, if only for a little while. Anyway, it's not like I ever had a burning desire to be a lawyer.

Of course, I wonder from time to time how my career would have evolved had I pursued that early dream. Regrets? Oh sure, maybe a few. You always wonder "what if?" But after my discharge from the Army, I wasn't thinking about any of that. I wanted to explore a different path, try something new. My first step took me to Wall Street.

Chapter 4

Baghdad by the Bay

Wall Street beckoned, and I responded. I landed a position with Edwards & Hanley, an established investment firm and a member of the New York Stock Exchange. It's a firm that's long since ceased to exist, having succumbed to industry consolidation, but at the time it was an exciting, energetic place, perfect—or so I thought—for a fresh-eyed kid seeking to make his mark in the challenging world of finance.

I immediately entered their training program for new salesmen. I had the look of a Wall Street go-getter. Well, sort of. Having been on a diet, courtesy of Uncle Sam's cuisine for the previous six months, my few suits hung on me like rags. I had a buzz cut, and while I was 23 years old, I probably looked no older than 14, especially in my baggy suits. But I was making $400 a month at Edwards & Hanley, working at 25 Broad Street in Lower Manhattan, the epicenter of the financial universe. What could be better?

I considered myself fortunate to launch my career in the busiest and most challenging business neighborhood in the world. Wall Street sat in the shadow of the new twin towers of the World Trade Center, which were completed during my years there. I started with the firm in March 1970, soon after my discharge from active duty. What I thought would be a meteoric rise soon became something else. Looking so much younger than my years placed me at a decided disadvantage in trying to persuade customers to join us. "Let's discuss your serious investment dollars, sir."

Over time, my initial enthusiasm for Wall Street waned. It was an enlightening experience, no doubt, but the early 1970s saw recession, which put a damper on the ability of Wall Street to fire its cylinders at full throttle. It exposed me to a world I didn't really embrace or understand, and it could be a very, very hard slog if you were 23 years old and had no family connections. A lot of my peers and competitors in that world were scions of wealthy families. Me? I was starting at square one.

In order to thrive, you worked hard. You cold-called prospective customers. Failure was the common result, no matter how skilled a salesman you were. There were many bumps and bruises, ups and downs, along the way. Not getting discouraged, learning how to handle rejection, those were useful experiences that continue to serve as professional life lessons. Wall Street offers a dramatic education in learning how to survive downturns and how to celebrate upturns. "Never get too high when you win or too low when you lose." That was one of Coach Broderick's favorite expressions from my high school basketball years.

I quickly found that being a salesman on Wall Street was a very personal, one-on-one undertaking. As someone schooled in the ways of teamwork from my basketball days in Bayonne, it was a new experience. You really are on your own. Sure, you have researchers working with you, there's back office support, and you can use the trading desk. More than anything else, though, it's about selling yourself, establishing your own credibility and connections with customers.

At the end of the day, the foundation of my approach to selling business and engaging customers was built in those three-plus years on Wall Street. Preparation, homework, communication—these are attributes of the successful salesman and of the successful business executive. These were the things—along with my friendship with Alan Ulan, my oldest and dearest friend—that I took away from Wall Street.

Wall Street wasn't nearly as sophisticated in the early 1970s as it is today. We were selling stocks, bonds, and mutual funds. There were no private equity or hedge funds in abundance back then or anything even remotely as complicated as the kind of financial products Wall Street administers today. I used to call customers at night at their homes; a lot of business got transacted that way. I worked primarily from the Edwards & Hanley offices in Paramus, New Jersey, where a typical day started around 8 A.M., lining up trades, soliciting new customers, and keeping the current ones happy.

Usually, when the markets closed at 4 P.M., I'd hop in my car and drive over to the nearby Hackensack YMCA for an hour of pick-up basketball. The Hackensack Y was a magnet for professional athletes; it wasn't uncommon to find myself in a game with New York Giants football stars like Spider Lockhart and Ron Johnson. After that, it was a quick shower and back to work. If I had a customer appointment, I'd usually get home between 8 and 9 P.M. If not, I'd work from my desk for several hours, cold calling.

I became a reasonably accomplished mutual funds salesman. E&H ran sales contests twice a year. If you sold a goal amount in mutual funds, you could qualify for a company trip for four or five days to places such as Puerto Rico, Mexico, or the Caribbean. My then-wife, Barbara, and I went on our share of company-subsidized trips, nice vacations.

Once, I opened more new accounts than anyone else over a defined period and won a color television set. Now, I couldn't afford a color TV on my own in 1972, so this was exciting. A few days later, we watched one of the most electrifying football plays in history—Franco Harris's immaculate reception for the Pittsburgh Steelers—in living color from the privacy of our home. Great stuff.

Yet, as the months passed, I felt as though I wasn't really building a career. I've always regarded myself as something of a builder, but I could just never envision Wall Street as a professional platform for my family and me. I guess I never thought of myself sitting on top of this particular world. In the spring of 1973, change was what I needed, and change was coming over the horizon at the tennis courts in Bayonne one Saturday afternoon.

Although Bayonne is a working-class city, it had built and maintained public tennis courts that were immaculate, gorgeous. Bayonne at the turn of the twentieth century had been a resort town, situated as it was off the scenic Hudson River and bordered as well by Newark Bay. Our magnificent clay courts were among the few remaining vestiges of that time. I was an avid player and spent as much time as I could there.

The guy who cared for them was named Phil. He was an employee of the Bayonne Parks Department and tended these courts as though they were precious jewels. He could be a bit of a grump, but for some reason he liked me and a few of my friends who had been regulars at the courts since we were kids. I had blond hair in my younger years, and Phil used to call me Whitey, as in "Givin' you Court No. 1 today, Whitey, star court!"

That afternoon, I ran into Michael Blitzer, an old high school friend. Michael had gone to work for an executive recruiting firm in New York. I hadn't seen him since our graduation from Bayonne High School, so we took a few minutes to catch up. How are things, what have you been up to? We exchanged the usual kinds of news.

"I'm working on something with this great company," he told me. "You ought to think about it." Michael went to work on my behalf. A few months later, I was a salesman for United States Leasing International, Inc. U.S. Leasing was the first American company whose core technology was equipment leasing. It had been established in 1954, when the leasing industry was going through a period of dramatic growth, a protracted period over which it became an enormous industry.

A few years out of Rutgers as a history major, and here I was shifting my professional interest to equipment leasing. I had no idea that it would become my chosen field for the rest of my career. A day or two after joining the company, I was told to attend a company sales conference at a convention center in Glen Cove, Long Island. The senior executives from U.S. Leasing flew out from the home office in San Francisco for the event, each scheduled to talk to the assembled group.

I showed up knowing no one, extremely wet behind the ears. I sat in the back of the auditorium as one speaker after another rose to discuss our business, our sales, our customers, and our vision for the future. To a man—and they were all men in those days—they came across as thoughtful and insightful. On top of that, they were utterly smooth, confident, and well spoken.

"When I grow up, I want to be like those guys," I remember telling myself. It was an inspirational moment. They were cool in a way that I was not, in total control of the material, establishing a powerful connection with their audience. The concept of being able to stand in front of a crowd like that and hit a home run was completely foreign to me. As a rookie in the leasing business, I was looking for my niche.

Since then, public speaking has become almost second nature. I now hope and believe there are times when I'm speaking to a large external audience or to one made up of our own people that some 20-something salesman in the back row is saying to himself, "That's who I want to be like when I grow up."

★   ★   ★

After that sales conference in 1973, I returned to my office at U.S. Leasing, a 26-year-old salesman learning the business. My sales turf was northern New Jersey. I wanted to absorb everything I could, not only about the territory but also about the products we were leasing. The education of all executives, from their earliest career moments through ascension to the C-suite if they're fortunate, is a process without end.

I've never been afraid to work hard, to take chances even at the risk of failure. I've never thought, "If I do this, it's the end of my career." I've always wanted to stay curious about new things. I've never wanted to work for somebody who couldn't teach me something. In fact, that's one of the most compelling things I've learned along the way. Working for people who helped me take my game to the next level or become a better leader intellectually or temperamentally was important. I keep this at the forefront of my mind, because now I'm the one doing most of the teaching. Constantly learning, absorbing, finding things that are interesting and engaging—that's what brings vitality to the workplace.

As I was starting to pick up leadership cues, my boss at the time was an important person in helping to shape my career. He was a guy named Jim Cain who had been a schoolteacher and brought an analytical, academic quality to his work. He could take a concept and break it down into three or four parts, then help you understand each part individually and in relation to the others. He was very articulate and had become very successful at a young age. I didn't know diddlysquat about the leasing business, and soon after I started working for him, Jim handed me three binders—the U.S. Leasing traditional Red, Green, and Blue Books. "Read these," he said. That was all we had at the time in way of training, pretty much. Three binders full of instructions on how to do the job. You hoped that you'd find someone who could really show you the ropes, take those written guidelines and help you succeed. Fortunately, I found that in Jim.

Jim wasn't a typical manager. He was loud and boisterous, a garrulous fellow with a wicked sense of humor and no hesitation about speaking his mind. (One of his favorite expressions was, "That guy is a GAPING asshole.") He was an early mentor, someone I respected and used for inspiration in later years.

Unfortunately, he was my boss for only a year before transferring to corporate headquarters in San Francisco. Jim and his wife eventually left California and moved to Australia, where he went to work for another company in the leasing business. In an ironic twist, while I was at AT&T years later, we acquired that company and Jim ended up working for me. Small world.

After several years in the field, I ended up at the home office myself.

The U.S. Leasing building in San Francisco was located on Battery Street, in what had been the warehouse district. In fact, the building had been an old mattress factory before it was redesigned for our use. It was a beautiful place, architecturally impressive and with high-ceilinged elevators. I thought at the time that I could be happy spending the rest of my days in San Francisco. I loved the sights, the food, and the people, especially Herb Caen.

Herb Caen was a columnist with the *San Francisco Chronicle* for several decades, a writer who knew the city well. With a nod to the legends of "1001 Arabian Nights," he used to refer to San

Francisco as "Baghdad by the Bay" for its renowned—even noto-rious—cultural and ethnic diversity. A collection of his essays published under that title won Caen the Pulitzer Prize for Commentary in 1996, a year before his death. The phrase sticks with me to this day; it summed up the city beautifully, and with humor.

Closer to home professionally, I had gotten to know Ben Maushardt, the CFO of U.S. Leasing. He was the embodiment of a caring, thoughtful corporate leader, one who understood nuance and how to motivate people effectively. I was transferred to the San Francisco office in January 1979, and given responsibility for deal analysis and interactions with potential investors and lenders on structured finance deals and other large, complex transactions that required a lot of analytical work and a broad business perspective.

I used a dumb terminal in those days, a kind of early computer terminal that had no intelligence. It was a device no bigger than a typewriter that transmitted data over telephone lines. Often, I'd take it home with me and work on it at night. The kids would be watching television, and there I would be, sitting in the den, hunkered down with my terminal, running the sawtooth debt structure or some other confounding analysis.

After my arrival at company headquarters, I realized I probably didn't have the academic grounding required to do the job as well as I'd like. Getting an MBA seemed a timely and appropriate idea, but this was the spring of 1979. I had been out of college for 11 years and had a wife and two kids. How could I possibly pull off a graduate education?

As it happens, Pepperdine University, one of the leading uni-versities on the West Coast and widely known and respected for its graduate programs, had created one of the first executive MBA programs in the country. I'd have the opportunity to attend classes a couple of weekends a month and for extended sessions during the summer, earning my degree and keeping my day job. But the weekend sessions required about 25 hours of preparation each week. It was a bear, beyond exhausting, but still an opportunity worth pursuing.

When I'd first looked into it, I found that the program would cost me $30,000. You might as well have said $300 million. I really wanted and needed to do this, I was convinced, but how to pay for it? U.S. Leasing had a tuition reimbursement program, but it wasn't anything to write home about: taking a course, college or graduate and business-related, an employee could receive $500 a year.

I had an idea, one I wasn't sure Ben would welcome. Nevertheless, I knocked on his door one day, explained my situation, and suggested a solution. I had been brought out to San Francisco, I pointed out, and given a new job that didn't perfectly fit my training and experience. Pepperdine has a great MBA program that fills the bill, I explained, and I want to enroll.

"The only problem," I said, "is that it costs $30,000."

Ben paused for a moment. "What do you want me to do about it?"

"I want the company to pay for it," I said.

Ben alluded to the company policy, that academic reimbursement was capped at $500 per year.

So I hit him with my best shot. "You obviously think I'm going somewhere in the company, and I'm telling you I'm lacking some of the quantitative skills I need. And I don't have anywhere near the $30K it will take to pay tuition.

"Okay," he said.

"Okay what?" was my response.

"You have a pretty good argument. I'll recommend it to Ned," he replied.

Now, this was not exactly what I wanted to hear. David E. Mundell—better known to all as Ned—was our chief executive officer and a legendary curmudgeon. I had been confident through the whole conversation with Ben until he invoked Ned. I was sure I would get fired once the question of full reimbursement was broached with Ned. A few days later, Ned's secretary called me and told me to stop by his office. This is it, I thought. I'm finished. Turned out I was wrong.

"Good idea," he said of the reimbursement proposal. I was a little stunned as he walked through the only condition attached to it. If I left the company within two years I would have to pay the money back, but otherwise the check would come without strings. "And I don't want to be bothered with this," he added. "We're going to give you the whole $30,000 upfront; you manage it."

A more typical meeting with Ned Mundell was quite an experience. A pipe smoker, he had a large rack of pipes on the credenza behind his desk. He'd be puffing on one, peering over his reading glasses at you, eyeing whatever paperwork you'd brought in for him to review. An engineer by education, he'd drag out his ancient Keuffel and Esser (K&E) slide rule when he was studying business cases. He wouldn't say anything, but he'd examine your printout, find something on, say, page 63, and point out "that number is wrong." You just wanted to scream.

A legendary curmudgeon, as I said, but still a stand-up guy. I think sometimes that the grumpy persona was a mask he liked to show the outside world. He was very smart, articulate, and could be really funny if caught in the right moment.

But clearly, Ben had gone to bat for me. He taught me an important lesson about how to manage and, more importantly, how to lead effectively. U.S. Leasing had maybe 1,000 employees, and here I was, a relatively junior member of the leadership team. Yes, I had been a successful salesman who earned a record of achievement during my six years. Yes, they had promoted me and brought me out west, giving me enhanced responsibilities. But it wasn't like I was a senior guy there. Ben went out on a limb for me.

Ben was an assertive leader, not a bureaucrat. He didn't spout the party line, didn't tell me I had brass ones for coming in with my proposal. He sat and listened, he weighed the arguments pro and con, then he decided on a course of action and made it happen. I think I've absorbed some of those habits over the years, and I have Ben to thank for demonstrating that brand of leadership. In fact, he had been one of the speakers years before who'd made such a lasting impression on me during that Glen Cove conference in my first week on the job with the company.

A Pepperdine postscript: When I graduated with my MBA two years later, I wanted to repay Ben for his support and the company's generosity. I bought him an American Express "Be My Guest" gift certificate for dinner and dropped it off with his secretary. "I appreciate all your support," my note read. He came by my office later and said he couldn't accept it. I talked him into it.

Two days later, he walked into my office. I was on the phone so he grabbed a yellow pad off my desk and began writing. "Doro's, Dom Perignon, lobster for two, crème brulée, etc. $495." Doro's was one of the most expensive restaurants in San Francisco back then. This was 30 years ago, when a $495 tab was off the charts. He turned without a word and walked out.

I'm sure I gulped back my response. I'd have to find the money somehow; I owed it and I owed him. When I finally got the Amex bill, it was actually $28. He and his wife had each had a couple of glasses of wine—and the last laugh on me.

★   ★   ★

After 11 years with one of the country's premiere leasing companies, I found myself drawn back to Wall Street, to the investment banking firm of Thomson McKinnon. While I loved just about everything about living in San Francisco and would have been happy to spend the rest of my days there, the Thomson offer was simply too good to turn down.

I had always told myself we would never leave the Bay Area unless I had the opportunity to make a lot more money in New York, move back to friends and family, and provide a better life for my wife and two young children. Thomson McKinnon's offer, frankly, blew me away—a far greater salary than I was making at U.S. Leasing, or could expect to earn there in the foreseeable future.

I soon learned, however, that Thomson McKinnon was an investment banking operation distinguished by being, well, undistinguished. Its struggles mounted and became more glaring in the years following my departure. In the late 1980s, a few years after I had left, the *Washington Post* described it as "a weak sister among the top 20 brokerage houses for years." I stayed only 13 months before leaving for AT&T.

When I arrived at Thomson, I quickly saw that it wasn't a well-run place. It didn't put any emphasis on collaboration; there was a palpable coolness and distance between the senior managers. It wasn't just the interpersonal work environment that concerned me, either. The firm was proficient in retail banking and deficient in investment banking, yet it was pumping additional resources into the investment banking side, which didn't seem an especially sound idea.

Stepping away from the core business—abandoning the essence of what makes a company viable and valuable—is something I've encountered again and again in my career. It's a strategy I've never quite understood, and I've always regarded that particular corporate behavior as at best a risky bet. Too often, chief executives either tire of doing the same thing, no matter how efficiently and well they do it, or they become enamored of the next big thing— even if it's a business strategy poorly conceived and doomed to failure from the outset. Frequently, we've seen radical changes in direction take a company over the cliff.

To this day, I have no regrets about taking the Thomson McKinnon job. I couldn't have realized it at the time I accepted the offer, but it paved my way for a better opportunity, with AT&T. (It's funny. With the exception of Hewlett-Packard, no company I've worked for is still around in its original form. Despite that, I think HP is safe—at least for the moment.)

However, I wasn't really searching for a way out when Tom Wajnert called in 1985. Tom had landed as COO of AT&T Credit Co., handling the finance and leasing business for AT&T. We'd been good friends and colleagues during our time together at U.S. Leasing. Tom needed a strong financial manager to help him build what he envisioned as an industry-leading captive finance company. Would I be interested in joining him? I jumped at the chance.

During my Thomson McKinnon days, I had realized with each passing month that my heart really was still in the leasing business. While Wall Street had made me an offer I couldn't refuse, it really wasn't where I wanted to be. Once before, I'd transitioned from Wall Street to a major leasing operation, and the results had been salutary. I hoped history was about to repeat itself.

Chapter 5

The AT&T
Rollercoaster

O ver the years, you begin to understand what drives you professionally, where your talents are best focused, what makes you good at what you do, and, perhaps most important, the thing that gets you out of bed in the morning and makes you feel like you can't wait to get to work. Wall Street had never done that for me. The leasing business had, and I was counting on AT&T Credit to do it again.

Mission accomplished. My years at AT&T were deeply satisfying, all in all, and career defining. I had come to the company at just the right moment, at the beginning of a new and exciting period. It was a magical time; our AT&T group was growing, the economy was booming, and we were buying companies and gobbling up business lines.

AT&T Credit had been formed to implement the parent company's decision to expand its telephone switch business. It was a sophisticated operation; the terminology was technical and specific and involved a different customer base, commercial enterprises. Two AT&T lines evolved to handle this emerging market. One was designed to serve larger, more complicated, multimillion-dollar business deals. The other was dedicated to smaller businesses, deals in the $5,000 range, for example, and there were potentially thousands of them.

There was a sense that we could do great things at AT&T. I think Tom wanted to recreate the U.S. Leasing conglomerate with the automobile leasing component, computer-leasing companies, and structured finance deals we'd done at our old place. He didn't explicitly tell anybody that was what he wanted to do, but it seemed clear to me, and he had a willing accomplice in Morris "Morry" Tannenbaum. Morry had been vice-chairman of AT&T and had recently stepped into the role of CFO. A veteran of the company, he understood the AT&T culture and mindset. He also had very impressive academic bona fides, with a PhD in physics.

I enjoyed him professionally and personally. He made me laugh at the most unpredictable times. We were financing telephone systems, of course, but we were also doing a lot of other financing.

We expanded into aircraft financing and had a small fleet of planes. At one point during our days together, when I was still CFO, a Hawaiian Airlines plane was forced to crash land. This was a high-cycle airplane, a short-hop craft that experienced enormous stress from a lot of takeoffs and landings. The *New York Times* reported that the incident had been attributed to pop rivets weakened by all the plane's ascents and descents.

The morning the *Times* article appears, I'm sitting at my desk. It's one minute past 8:00. The phone rings. It's Morry.

"Good morning," I said.

The hint of anxiousness in his voice was palpable. "Irv," he asked me, "do our planes have pop rivets?" This was top of mind that particular morning for Morry.

He was a terrific executive and an extremely smart guy. To me, he seemed almost heroic, championing our cause to a corporate leadership that was still wary of what we were about and what we could achieve. He carried our banner at the most senior levels of the corporation, where he wielded considerable influence. Morry got it. He realized that AT&T Credit had created its own platform, was being run by talented, innovative executives, and was making money while at the same time furnishing tax shelter for the parent company. Stand back and let them do what they do; that was his message to the brass.

I was the CFO of AT&T Credit, Tom's number two. I was learning a lot about the capital markets side of the business, interacting with interesting people. My work seemed to eat up eight days a week, 25 hours a day, but I loved every minute of it. During one period around Christmas, we were negotiating to purchase a company. It was a complicated, detailed process, and we ended up working a couple of successive all-nighters. The next night, I was supposed to attend a holiday function that was more or less an industry must do, a black-tie affair.

Though exhausted and wanting to do just about anything else, I told my secretary, "Get me a stretch limo." She asked why, because this request really was out of character for me.

"I'll sleep all the way up and all the way back." The dinner was about ninety minutes north of our office, so it wasn't exactly the most restful trip. It was an exhilarating time, to be sure.

As part of the build-up of the business, we needed a back office, which is how we ended up outsourcing the small-customer business to Chase. And that was what led us to Paul Gustavson and the implementation of a business model that helped redefine how captive finance companies operate.

Life was good. Still, there were challenges and intriguing developments along the way. Most were managerial, but one was physical. In December 1987, I hurt my back. I didn't know what it was initially. All I knew was that I had this pain in my butt. I didn't think much of it at the time, but it kept getting worse. After the first of the year, I went to see a friend of mine who happened to be an orthopedist. An MRI disclosed a herniated disk. We all wanted to avoid surgery, so I was ordered to bed for three weeks.

I couldn't get up except for a quick shower and short bathroom breaks. I took all my meals in bed—three meals a day, seven days a week. Trust me, it's not what it's cracked up to be. My wife had a teaching job and was gone most of the day, though we had a live-in housekeeper who could assist me during the hours Barbara was gone. I had a silver whistle, the kind used by basketball coaches and referees.

Our housekeeper would come running when I whistled that I needed something. Sometimes I would shout as she ascended the stairs, "Number 14, we got you for blocking, two shots!" She had no idea what I was talking about, but I had to amuse myself in some way. If mimicking a basketball referee did the trick, so be it.

This was no time to be away from the office. We were just too busy to be without the CFO for an extended period. So fax machines, speakerphones, and similar gadgets were installed in my bedroom. People came in for meetings with me in my pajamas. Even though I was slowed by my injury, the pace of our work never was. I figured after three weeks I'd be up and around, ready to reconquer the world. It was not to be.

The back didn't improve; in fact, it got much worse. My friend Eddie Decter, the orthopedist, took over and surgery was scheduled at St. Barnabas Medical Center in Livingston, New Jersey, one of the best hospitals in the area. Eddie personally selected the neurosurgeon and the anesthesiologist, and we prepared for the procedure. Besides being a world-class orthopedist, Eddie held a quirky distinction. His college roommate at the University of Maryland had been Larry David, co-creator of *Seinfeld* and later *Curb Your Enthusiasm*. Whenever you see an old *Seinfeld* episode and there's a doctor in it, his name is Dr. Decter in homage to our mutual friend.

The herniated section was removed from my spine in January 1988, and I was back to work about eight days later. I really couldn't wait to return to the office; to say I was a little stir crazy at home would be an understatement. Near the end of my recuperation at home, Tom Wajnert came for a visit. We had lunch at the dining room table, cold cuts for the two of us, me in my pajamas and robe. It was the first time Tom had been to see me since I was ordered to bed, but he had a proposal that needed to be discussed face to face.

"Irv," he said, "I want you to take day-to-day responsibility for our business units." Under his plan, I would in effect be in charge of each of the various AT&T Credit businesses—leasing, automotive, IT. Tom wanted to step back from daily management of the businesses in order to devote more energy to strategy and M&A. Tom was an enormous guy—6′4″, maybe 300 pounds—and he had ambition to match. Buying companies and becoming a player on Wall Street really appealed to him.

That was all well and good, except for one thing. None of his direct reports, the team I was supposed to be directing, would actually be reporting to me. He intended to withhold the power to manage.

He wanted me to conduct the business reviews, to concentrate on their performance. "Well, Tom, how am I going to do that?" I asked. How would I be able to tell these guys what to do when they could all do an end run around me to the CEO's office? The challenges were mostly interpersonal. From an organizational standpoint, they still reported to Tom, but they de facto reported to me. We had the vendor-leasing business, our captive finance business, automobile financing business, and the information technology business, and now they all would be part of my world.

Here I was, recuperating from major surgery to mend an ailing back, and I was heading back to a role that would, I was sure, bring me lots of additional discomfort. I was CFO at the time. The CFO usually does CFO things, not this. But Tom knew I was tough enough and smart enough to do it. He wanted to assure ongoing oversight, and he didn't want to pick one of the other guys. So he picked the guy with no business unit. It was a very uncomfortable situation, and it lasted until 1991, when I was promoted to president and Chief Operating Officer of AT&T Credit Corp.

★   ★   ★

My challenges weren't all physical or supervisory, of course. As Tom's right-hand man, I would occasionally butt heads with him. There's a natural friction between any CEO and CFO, particularly when the two are motivated from time to time by differing ideas about how to manage the business. Many times, I had to decide whether to get with the program or speak my mind, even if the consequences might be grave. I'm not the kind to sit meekly in the back of the room, nodding in support of every plan that emerges from the chief executive's office.

At AT&T Capital, we were financing the company from the outside. We didn't inhibit AT&T's access to capital, although that had been the perception in some quarters. The monopoly guys, from the old days, had their doubts about us almost from the start. We raised money externally, though; we generated tax shelter, and we produced profit. All in all, our performance was creditable.

One crucial lesson I've learned is that you must add value. Customers will pay you for something they need that will benefit them and their business in tangible ways. The last thing they want to pay you for is a commodity. If you can't demonstrate value, success can remain elusive. In meetings to this day, I find myself talking about whether we have a real value proposition and are not just a pot of money.

Our time at AT&T started in the go-go 1980s—I could never understand the issue that AT&T corporate had with us. We weren't buying other companies or service lines for billions of AT&T dollars. Everything we bought was purchased with money from outside the business. It was really no big deal as long as we continued to generate tax shelter for them—which we did, and profitability—which we did. We covered our own expenses. We helped them sell product. Perfectly sensible.

Was there resentment of the new kids on the block? No, not really. AT&T had started a credit-card business, AT&T Universal—I still have my card, all these years later. This was a business started not by us, but by them. People could use cards to make phone calls, and AT&T had this huge consumer face, so that was the whole idea behind it. They were raising money outside the business, as well.

I went to AT&T executive leadership. We generate tax shelter, I pointed out, they generate taxable income. We finance outside the business, they finance outside the business. Why don't we combine the entire financial business into one entity? I proposed. It would be a smash hit. Didn't happen. They were old school executives—no, we're not going to do it. That was the mantra. It could have made them even more powerful, but no, they weren't interested. It was a shame, really.

But, thanks to support from Morry and others in leadership at AT&T, we had been allowed to grow organically and through acquisitions. It was a hectic period. In fact, we were on a bit of a merger and acquisition binge. Around 1990, Tom said that he wanted to acquire an IT leasing company whose CEO was a close friend of his.

As negotiations proceeded, things deteriorated. The other side continued to re-trade the deal, always to our detriment. Although nervous about raising their concerns with the boss, our mergers and acquisitions (M&A) team wanted out of this deal. They thought it was too risky and its assumptions so extreme that it could even bring down the company. I had no involvement in the deal—Tom was handling this one personally—but one day I got a call from the team asking me to intercede. Despite the evidence that it had become an abysmal mess, Tom still wanted to proceed.

I had no interest in sticking my nose into this hornet's nest, but I did, reluctantly. Even though no one ever seeks to be in the boss's crosshairs, this was a critical juncture for us. If the dire predictions were accurate, this could cause devastating damage to the company. I called Tom and asked him to meet me at our Morristown, New Jersey, headquarters the following Saturday morning. That day, he entered the room, me at the table flanked by a couple of members of the M&A team.

"Tom," I began, "we can't do this deal. It's a disaster. Nobody around this table wants to do it." The deal was a loser, I explained. We were paying too high a price, they were way overvalued, and we were taking virtually all of the risk. No way were we going to make this deal work; there was nothing about this analysis that made anybody feel good.

Of course, Tom protested. He never raised his voice, though I could tell he was clearly upset with our collective and pointed dissent. He insisted that we were making a mistake, but the following Monday, he called the other side and canceled the deal.

It was a risky decision for me to step into the middle of this issue, especially since it involved Tom's close friend, a guy I knew and liked as well. Frankly, I didn't know exactly how it would play out. Angering your boss when it could derail you from your career path should always give one pause. Ultimately, that shouldn't be the overriding factor. Sometimes you just have to play gutsball. You've got to do the right thing. I've never been afraid of consequences. I knew it was the right thing to do, and Tom and I survived this episode. In the end, we were vindicated. The other company effectively ran its portfolio under; we had dodged a bullet.

Not buying a company was the exception in those days, or so it seemed. Some of the acquisitions we made didn't exactly get off to rousing starts. If you don't do the transition and implementation work effectively, you might find yourself playing catch-up from the start. Strategically, we were in the hunt for smaller, more established companies that would fit nicely into our universe, or provide us a complementary entree to an industry in which we had little historical presence.

One vendor leasing company we purchased during our buying blitz was a perfect example. It allowed us to apply the skills we had acquired as a captive to customer financing for other businesses, in this case manufacturing. We also bought an automobile fleet leasing company. That one bombed. It was one of those decisions based more on instinct and personal relationships than cold, objective fact checking and due diligence.

One of the things I learned during my days at AT&T was that networking and personal relationships are useful. They can help forge profitable connections in the business world. But they can't be the foundation for multimillion-, even billion-dollar deals. If the numbers don't square, and the upside isn't clear after extensive review and consideration, walk away.

★   ★   ★

We'd built this tremendous rocket ship, launched it, and watched our fortunes rise with it. The company had grown organically, externally, and quite rapidly. In 1991, our assets were in the neighborhood of $9 billion. Over the next five years, we had projected they'd double in value. That's what we told AT&T when we put our five-year plan on the table.

But the senior leadership at AT&T didn't like the idea of having a big finance company. They went to Alex Mandl, the CFO of AT&T at the time, and told him he should try to find some way to modify the AT&T ownership structure. At that point, the dominoes were teetering. I saw this coming and came up with a plan I was sure would provide the kind of protection we needed. I took my idea to Tom.

"Maybe we can get them off our back if we say we're going to borrow money on our own, without any parent company participation whatsoever," I said. We were borrowing money, and AT&T was assuring lenders there would be fixed-charge coverage of it. It was tantamount to a guarantee. I was suggesting we do away with the AT&T guarantee.

The company known as AT&T Capital arose from that initial conversation. We constructed a holding company, and all of our assets and entities would become wholly owned subsidiaries of AT&T Capital. We were going to be the direct borrower. Instead of a guarantee, we'd get Wall Street to accept a $1 net-worth agreement. AT&T told Wall Street that the net worth of AT&T Capital would never fall below a dollar, still a de facto guarantee, but one with far less onerous implications in the eyes of the AT&T leadership cadre.

Everything depended upon us earning an A bond rating, so that AT&T would be comfortable that we could borrow money cheaply enough to support AT&T products with leasing services, competitively priced. Nevertheless, our corporate leaders were still worried. The assets of AT&T Capital were becoming significant compared to the rest of the company's assets. There was concern that The Street might start to look at AT&T as a blended multiple. Common stock of finance companies typically trade at a 10-ish multiple. That means the stock price will be 10 times per share earnings (e.g., $1.00/share earnings × 10 = $10.00 stock price). Industrials like AT&T typically trade at much higher multiples, 20 or higher. Hence, the concern on the part of the AT&T senior guys; nobody wanted to see AT&T trading at 15 times earnings.

Our thinking was that we would do a small IPO. We wanted to maintain tax consolidation and establish a trading range for the stock. The plan was to sell 14 percent of the company to investors, retain about 6 percent of the stock for senior AT&T Capital management, and preserve the rest for AT&T. From the end of the first quarter of 1991 until August 1993, when we actually traded our first shares on the New York Stock Exchange, it was all about getting ready for the IPO. Everything else got shoved to the side. The corporate attitude was "Let's get the company ready for the IPO. We don't care what it takes to do it; just do it."

By 1993, AT&T Capital was a company with more than $11 billion in assets. We had shared with AT&T's senior leadership a business plan that projected growth to $25 billion in assets over the next few years. But the older executives were hardened in their views of the world, most of them alumni of the Bell Systems network that regarded anything without a dial tone as useless. They weren't interested in a blended multiple, not one iota. I didn't blame them, but I didn't think their reasoning was sound, either. It was infuriating. You'd talk to people on Wall Street, and they'd say they didn't give a hoot about finance company debt; it was collateralized, relatively short-term, with an established credit history. The blended multiple scare was bunk as well; AT&T Capital's contribution to earnings was minimal.

It was tough running the business during the time leading up to the IPO. We had to keep operating efficiently while at the same time preparing the business for sale.

This whole situation was out of my hands. You can influence what you can control, and over this, I had no control. Our task was to get the public offering completed. Then, I was certain, we could get back to the business of doing what we loved to do. But we had to deal with the IPO and Wall Street expectations in the meantime. So we prepared for the IPO, got the IPO ready, reacted to the IPO, dealt with the fallout from the IPO. It was all-IPO, all the time. Even after we went public, it still felt like everything associated with the public offering was overwhelming our efforts to make the company better.

In 1995, it all came crashing down. AT&T had decided to divest itself of NCR. NCR was launched in 1884 as the National Cash Register Company, makers of the first mechanical cash register. We'd bought NCR, now a data processing and storage operation, in 1991. It was never anything but a disaster for AT&T. In 1994, NCR's name was changed to AT&T Global Information Solutions, or GIS. Another highly questionable choice.

Why would anyone buy a 100-year-old brand, recognized and respected around the world, and change its name? And change it to a techno babble name that meant nothing? Thinking about it, I guess I can understand such a head-shaking move. After all, this is the same creative process that produced Lucent.

When AT&T acquired NCR, NCR Credit Corp. was a sleepy little credit subsidiary. We talked our AT&T parent into "selling" NCR Credit to us for the princely sum of one dollar. As it turned out, we didn't overpay by much. Once it came to us, it reported to me, and I spent a lot of time in Dayton, Ohio, where NCR's headquarters were located. I remember being in Dayton for a meeting where I listened to AT&T corporate people talk about the rationale for changing the company name from NCR to AT&T Global Information Solutions.

The NCR folks could not believe it. They were stunned into silence. Changing the name of a business that, for good or bad, is a widely recognized brand name is lunacy. They may be going through difficult times, but they still have the name. It makes you scratch your head. Years later, Mark Hurd, whose early career was at NCR and who served as CEO of Hewlett-Packard in the 2000s, and I would go round and round on this idea while we were both at HP, as if it was my fault that AT&T had made such an obviously bone-headed choice.

AT&T decided to rid itself of GIS and take a sizeable book loss—the name reverted to NCR in 1996 to facilitate purchase as an independent, publicly traded company. Side by side was the intent to spin off its telephone switch business—to then Lucent, now Alcatel Lucent. There was no further need for a captive finance company. Once the divestiture decision was finalized, AT&T came to us and said "Here, you do it. Put yourselves on the block." That placed us in a position of propping ourselves up for sale and working toward initiating and completing a deal ourselves. There's something a little strange about being told to sell yourself. It took us a long time to finish the deal.

We worked with the investment banks on the offering memorandum. It took us six to eight weeks to get the book ready, and we were running into the December 1995 holidays. We began entertaining prospective buyers at due diligence meetings in January 1996. During five months, we must have conducted more than 15 due diligence sessions. People would come in for an entire day, or two or three. In May, we finally struck a deal.

Guy Hands, now head of the private equity firm Terra Firma but then managing director at Nomura Securities Company, Ltd., the big Japanese investment bank, bid an acceptable price based on what I believed was a dubious financial plan. A spokesman said AT&T was "very satisfied and pleased with the outcome." That made one of us.

At the time, it was one of the largest leveraged buyouts in U.S. business history, an impressive transaction by any standard, regardless of how I felt about it personally. I was unhappy about how the whole process had transpired. It was an exhausting time for all of us. I was worried about my team and how it would affect their futures. In any event, deal done.

Hands's approach was to securitize receivables to pay for the purchase. They put a price on the table, a pretty good price. He paid $45 a share, far more than double the opening price when we had gone public only two years earlier. Some people pay for things by breaking the company apart. He wanted his money out right up front, taking a real private-equity approach.

From there, I had to assess my future. I had little interest in transitioning to the new company; that was certain. But Hands didn't give up easily. He invited me to dinner to talk, even though I was transmitting signals that I wasn't planning to stay. They had offered me a lot of money and a big bump in salary, but the job I would want in order to stay wasn't what they had in mind. The new position would be a significant reduction in responsibility, particularly as it related to the international business—and international business was where the world was heading. To be left out of it was unacceptable.

★   ★   ★

Once the sale was announced, we, as a senior management team, hired Joseph Batchelder to assist us in working out financial packages with the new owner. Batchelder was the premier attorney in the New York metropolitan area on personal contract matters for corporate executives. Very professorial. Tom brought him on board to protect our interests, collectively and individually. Tom did very well; he got trains, planes, automobiles, and handsome bonuses. As it turned out, Batchelder really only represented him. The rest of us were on our own, not that we did poorly, mind you.

The deal closed in October 1996. In the months prior, the atmosphere at AT&T Capital was poisonous. All kinds of bad feelings had developed during this very taxing period. Everybody was concerned about his or her own thing, cutting separate deals. We devolved from a team that I thought had a real sense of shared mission to one that was distrustful and divisive. Most decided to stay. Dan McCarthy, our legal counsel, and I were the only ones in the senior leadership group who decided we had no interest in being a part of the new company.

Our message to them was this: We aren't going to tender our shares; we'll stay a few months and help in the transition if you want us to. Strangely enough, around this time I had a dream that I saved Dan's life by pulling him from a car to safety after a flash flood. But had I? It was the two of us against the world, or at least that's how it felt.

Hands wanted to maintain some continuity, so he kept Tom on for a time before cutting him loose. The new company had started to do badly. You can't take $3.5 billion in receivables out of an asset base and expect to do well. And you can't grow fast enough to make up the difference. Say you have $12 billion, and you lose $3.5 billion. How do you get right back to $12 billion? In our business, assets amortize away even as you add new ones to the portfolio. You have to write double the amount of new volume to close such a gap—$7 billion, we are talking real money. The assumptions were way too aggressive.

Still, during our dinner to discuss the future, he persisted.

"Look," he said, "I really can't have you leave the company. Tom's my horse, and I'm riding him, but I need a backup." He bought a very expensive bottle of wine. I tasted it, then didn't drink another drop all night, me the oenophile.

"Son," I said, "you're riding the wrong horse."

He was upset with me and probably with the idea that a valued high-level member of Tom's team was refusing to cross the transom with him. It wasn't 100 percent clear when we parted ways that night, but I knew in my heart that it was the end.

Chapter 6

It's Got to Be
about the Customer

I left AT&T armed with over a decade of senior-level leadership experience. There was much to be proud of; I'd been a crucial part of growing a captive finance company that stood as one of the best in the business by the time Guy Hands closed his deal. It had been a great ride (for at least half my tenure there), and it had afforded me the opportunity to, in effect, run a big business—an invaluable experience and one I wouldn't trade for anything I've done in my career.

As I left AT&T, I felt I was well positioned to become a CEO somewhere. That would come in short order. But as I walked away from AT&T Capital for the last time, I realized that perhaps the most valuable thing I carried with me from my old business wasn't the healthy severance package, or the respect of my leadership team and industry peers.

No, it was the business model. Literally. Our operating model, the one whose seeds were planted so many years before in that Paramus diner with Paul Gustavson and those young hard chargers of mine, had matured into a blueprint not only for guiding a multibillion financial services company but for managing any group of people and motivating them to do their best work.

We had decided to redesign the business on the fly after that fateful get-together with Gustavson. Gerri Gold and Jim Tenner, two of my most trusted leaders, who had gotten me to take the Gustavson meeting in the first place and worked with me to start implementing the new model.

At its core, we realized, any new operating model had to be designed by the people closest to the customer. The customer was our business—and our people interacting with them daily—be they ops, sales, or whatever—knew best what the customer wanted and needed and would be willing to spend to acquire. That's the key to ensuring that any new business model will succeed and I can point to a few basic, incontrovertible principles that can spell the difference.

First, our goal is make a customer a customer for life. This is a core principle of mine, and I drive everyone around me a little bit crazy with it. Everything about how I conduct our business, the fiber that binds my leadership style and substance, is geared toward our customers.

We've made customer loyalty a rallying point. One of the things we want to emphasize with our people is that everything we do is designed to maintain alignment with the customer. In return, we want to nurture an equal sense of customer loyalty to us. Are customers willing to do business with us again? Or would they prefer to do business with someone else in the marketplace? Worst case, are they ambivalent about us and how we operate?

You never want a fifty-fifty attitude from your customers. That leaves you in a precarious state where anything could tip the scales toward their joining the ranks of former customers. We need to work constantly to transition our customers from ambivalence to a complete satisfaction. We need to get our customers on board and to bring them on board with enthusiasm. Of course, like most businesses catering to customers, we conduct satisfaction surveys. In our case, they're administered quarterly. Our compensation systems are constructed on the premise that high levels of customer satisfaction deserve higher employee compensation. There is an absolute correlation for customer satisfaction and profitability. Everyone is responsible for satisfying the customer, but organizations take their cues from the top.

That's why our executive team and I have added customer satisfaction components into the mix when determining our incentive compensation plans—and they're designed to cascade throughout the entire organization from us. While we've tinkered around the edges over the years, the customer-in foundation remains intact and at the very heart of our operating philosophy.

*   *   *

With the customer at the very top of our minds, we went to AT&T leadership in the early days and told them how we were going to enact our version of the "customer-in" philosophy. Our business was going to be designed from the customer in, having our customers determine, more or less, the kind of business we would be. We would establish a steering committee of maybe five people, and the steering committee would establish just a few key principles. We would create a design team, consisting of volunteers from different functions across the company, who would run with the steering committee's statement of principles. The perspective of all who expressed an interest in participating would be represented at the table; this was crucial to building out the model and assuring success.

The design team should be no more than 10 or 12 people, we decided. And it should meet consistently with the steering committee to ensure that any conclusions would be in conformance with the operating principles we had established.

The principles were straightforward business rules. One of them was "you can't design something that will cause us to blow the business plan out of the water." That wasn't the exact wording, of course, but it conveys the essence of what we were thinking. Proposals not only had to incorporate innovative thinking but also had to be grounded in solid business philosophy. We weren't about to relocate the company to Timbuktu, for example. Whatever was going to be designed had to be in full alignment with fundamental operating principles.

Our guidance to the team was that, as long as you remain true to the principles, whatever you design will be adopted. "You are not making a recommendation," we told the participants. "You are *truly designing the business.*" This group was truly empowered. These were the people closest to our customers, and they were going to determine how the business would operate.

Another core principle was that our people would share directly in the wealth they created. If they exceeded plan goals, it would be reflected in their compensation. Everyone in the organization was notified that we were going to hold an open selection process for positions on the design team. It wasn't up to me who would be chosen.

There would be no reaching out to recruit the team ourselves. You had to want to be on the design team; you had to tell us you wanted to be on the design team; and then you had to tell us how you could add value. With an open selection process and more candidates than positions, of course, not everyone who applied was going to make the team. Some, unfortunately, wouldn't make the cut.

The team was directed to spend about 50 percent of its time designing a better-aligned, re-energized operating system. They visited customer sites, company offices, and AT&T equipment salesman to assess their needs. They hosted *kaffee klatches* with their peers and colleagues and conducted hundreds of interviews with AT&T Credit employees. Those they didn't meet with directly, face to face or by phone, received questionnaires. They also set up a voicemail process to hear comments from interested co-workers.

As one of our team members later told the *New York Times* for its 1991 feature on our business model, they wanted to be a filter for everybody's needs.

The design team took all of this good input, separated the wheat (constructive ideas) from the chaff (gripes and whines), ran it up the flagpole during a series of meetings, and then put together a workflow analysis. From this very extensive review process, the team picked up ways to boost productivity and cut costs. For example, they figured we were losing millions of dollars a year through accounting inaccuracies and misplaced checks. Other losses in the millions, they estimated, resulted from poor or delayed credit decisions.

I had been surprised by the number of applicants to serve on the design team; about 60 people expressed firm interest in participating. The steering committee asked each to prepare a short essay on how to reorganize AT&T Credit. Fewer than half the applicant pool made it through the first cut to qualify for interviews with the steering committee, who chose 10 finalists based on their ability to work with each of our groups and dig up salient information.

That was pivotal. Our selection criteria had importantly included a demonstrated ability to work collaboratively with other members and a capability to bring to the discussions some sense of the business beyond their little corner of the world. We told them they would be able to travel to other offices and to hold sessions in different parts of the country, in different offices, with different groups, backgrounds, and perspectives.

At that time, we were primarily a U.S. business. We'd only begun in the late 1980s, to stick our toe into global business waters. We never intended for the design to be applied only to a U.S.-centric business. At the time, however, that was pretty much what we were. Our plan to take our business model and expand it globally was still in an embryonic state.

There were cultural implications, business practice implications. In some countries, the society itself is extraordinarily hierarchical, as is the business environment, and here we were, creating the "self-managed" team. A lot of people weren't quite sure what to do with that, how to bridge what might become gaps, even insurmountable obstacles, as we inevitably spread our operating vision to a more global stage.

We took the position, and still do, that people are people. Our feeling was that people used to working in a hierarchical style would embrace the model once they saw the customer reaction. I had faith that once we completed our design implementation for the U.S. business, it would travel well abroad eventually. There was no universal guarantee, of course. In Ireland, they immediately took to this model. That wasn't the case in Japan, by comparison.

★ ★ ★

The redesign process took a while. We were blazing new trails. It was very labor intensive. Every process we had was written on this thing called a variance chart. Literally, it was a chart that covered the back wall of a small conference room. The idea was to control variances at the source. In order to understand how to control variances at the source, we had to understand the whole process of where and how variances occurred.

It's critical to remember that this was more than an efficiency process, though. It was about superior customer service and *out-executing the other guy*. We were trying to simplify our operations processes, trying to shorten the steps from start to finish, while still maintaining control-process integrity. Where we might have had 25 or 30 steps to guide us through the life cycle of a transaction, we narrowed the number of steps down to 13. But it was 13 steps devised under three basic categories—put on, put through, and take off.

"Put on" was the part of the cycle that began when somebody actually sold something. That entailed a credit analysis and contract analysis before the deal finally was booked. "Put through" was the next phase, managing the process throughout the life of the deal. It involved customer invoicing, applying cash, dealing with various operations factors, satisfying our 80 zillion taxing authorities and tax mandates.

This was exactly what companies in our business didn't do well then and still don't today. There are always mistakes, always customer dissatisfactions. I remember our information technology guy used to come talk to me in the early days about some of the challenges of our system. He was always going on about bits and bytes. I always had to lie down when he left, because I got dizzy listening to him.

"I don't care what you do," I would tell him (and anyone else who needed to know), "you've got to bill, collect, and apply cash in a timely, accurate fashion. Then we'll be way ahead of the rest of the business. Customer satisfaction will go through the roof. Do the simple stuff right, get it right the first time, get it right on time, and you will have a leg up on the competition."

It's taken us almost 20 years—from AT&T Capital through Compaq Financial Services to present-day Hewlett-Packard Financial Services—to get it right. I'm a tough, demanding critic, but I have to say: I think we do it very well.

The third piece was "take off." That's what happens at the end of the lease. Is the product returned or purchased? Is a new leasing arrangement struck? Sounds simple, but when you're dealing with lots of little widgets, thousands of schedules, packing, crating, and delivering, it can become an extremely complicated process. We're still continually seeking to improve end of lease. It's hard for everyone in this line of work. When you're in the Information Technology business, you have to put a schedule on the books—90 million widgets, and 90 million schedules.

Anybody who runs a leasing company that does, say, $100 million a year, buys an off-the-shelf system, and they're good to go. We do closer to $100 million a day. We've got $12 billion on the balance sheet. And we're completely global today, in more than 50 countries. Complexity heaped upon complication. Life was so much simpler then, when this operating model was hatched, when were just a U.S.-centric business.

★   ★   ★

We got a lot of pushback from the rank and file and a lot from the executive team at AT&T. Every time we had a bad month, somebody would throw up their hands and say "Oh, this is a stupid idea." Socio-Tech. Yes, but this is what is going to get us where we wanted to go. Tom had told me to "go fix it" whenever the previous model needed improvement. So I fixed it. When it became successful, everybody loved it.

The real convincing had to be done at the corporate level. We fought with AT&T over many elements of the plan, particularly our ideas for compensating the team in accordance with the wealth creation model. As nature abhors a vacuum, large, powerful, and conservative corporations abhor significant change. In this case, the AT&T comp people wanted to keep everything consistent across the wage and salary spectrum. They couldn't accept a compensation proposal that wasn't aligned with that of the rest of the company.

And, of course, we were asking for the complete opposite. Don't impose a compensation structure on us that runs counter to the very essence of our new operating principles. Convincing them took a little time. We had lots of skirmishes with HR, and I've got more than a few scars to show from that period. (I always find it ironic when someone who has never run a business tries to tell me how to run mine.)

Soon after we implemented the model, however, we were planning to go global. If you operate on the premise of people managing themselves, allowing for individual group self-management within the overall parameters of the business plan, then it takes on a new level of challenge when you branch out into countries with different cultures, languages, business sensibilities, and management styles. You're talking about people managing themselves, equipped with a list of objectives. We would give them the list of objectives, and they would decide how to achieve them.

The business was broken down into a multiple teams of 12, 14, or 18 people, each deciding how to deploy its resources to achieve its goals. We provided them with a system to track their daily progress, how they were performing against their plan. This was called the *wealth creation model*—one of our key principles was to share the wealth with people who created the wealth. If you were working with the customer, putting the deal on the books, collecting the accounts, and earning revenue on those deals, you were helping to create the wealth.

Under our business model, employees would be subject to a separate compensation plan, with a quarterly payout. They got incentives based upon exceeding the plan. Our wealth creation model planted a series of markers along the way for our employees to pass—volume, of course, as well as turnaround time, collections, and delinquencies were several of our key objectives.

Looking back, I think about how basic it seemed, establishing these performance objectives. Almost too obvious. Yet you'd be amazed at how many companies don't do it. When we set targets for the wealth creation model, everything tied into what we were trying to do as a company. It wasn't as though they were supposed to do this, and the company was supposed to do something else.

At bottom, I wanted to make sure that everything was systemically linked. I did not want one thing that didn't make complete sense in terms of what we were trying to do. And I didn't want to make exceptions. Things would be hard as we ramped up our new model. We were asking a lot of our teams. This wasn't their father's corporate model—they were running the business in critical ways, not me. I would acknowledge that it was difficult, but we had to figure out how to do it anyway. Our competition wasn't sitting back and gently nudging the door open for us. They were playing hardball, using their operations capabilities to try to put us out of business. So when someone would come to me and ask, "Can we take the easy way just this one time, can we ignore the principles of our business?" My answer was no, consistently.

Our message had to be clear and unambiguous. Because if you said to your people, just this one time we're going to do this differently, the people were likely to think that there would always be a next time, another chance for the next shoe to drop. And our system would be more or less frozen: This is what they said, this is what they claim they want us to do, but they've changed the rule in this case and they say it's just this time and.... Well, that philosophy just won't fly.

I always placed my stock in "here's what the principles are, here's what has to get done, here is how it is systemically linked, this is the path we will follow." It doesn't necessarily mean we can't make adjustments. Rigidity for its own sake doesn't work either.

Adjusting against the principles we've created for our business across the board is open to regular review. But the proposed changes have to make sense, they have to work in the context of our principles-based work structure, and they can't be changed arbitrarily on a case-to-case basis.

I wanted our people to understand the rationale for doing certain things. I couldn't have the IT leader doing one thing when the company is going in a different direction. I couldn't abide the finance department working out of balance with the rest of the senior leadership.

We rolled out our new model region by region over a six-month period. It took about a year for it to take root throughout the organization, but it definitely took hold. You could see a palpable change in the way our team performed and in their individual attitudes toward their assignments and the company.

This was nothing less than employee ownership of the business—maybe not the Green Bay Packers kind of public ownership, but the kind that indisputably empowered employees. By working hard at outperforming the competition, they had a chance for career advancement and higher pay.

I often used to go to the office on Saturday and wander down to the floor where most of them would be working on any given weekday. I'd find many of them there, on the phone, working on documentation. They were coming in on their days off and in surprising numbers. And, I'm not just referring to folks in ops. We had lawyers, marketing people, finance types . . . in short, across the board participation. That told me they were highly motivated and feeling fully connected to the new program.

Capitalism at its best, to my way of thinking.... Give your people financial and organizational incentives, and they will respond by giving their absolute best in return. It's hard to believe, considering that halfway through my first lunch with Gustavson in 1986 I was ready to dismiss him as a communist loon. This was a full 180° pivot.

You get what you design for—that was Gustavson's message. I think our results through the years have been testament to that principle. It would serve me well as I entered into the next phase of my life: CEO of Compaq's new financial services unit.

Chapter 7

A Seat at the Head of the Table

There was something bittersweet about moving on to the next step in my professional journey after the AT&T Capital sale closed. How could there not be a range of mixed emotions, after I had been instrumental in creating a new financial services company from the ground floor and helping turn it into a multi-billion-dollar success story?

It was decision time for many of our executive team. Most of the AT&T Capital senior management team wanted to stay. Not me. I had made money, but I never really *had* money. We had taken a small percentage of the company in 1993, six or seven of us, and we'd be getting some sizable checks. For the time being, I had stuff. I was comfortable. Now I had free time.

I examined my life and my career, wondering about my next step. And I realized that I had spent the last 11 years of my career giving my blood, sweat, toil, and tears to AT&T Capital. I had equipment installed in my bedroom after back surgery and continued to work. I didn't want to be a party now to their stripping out more than $3 billion in receivables and gutting the company. I would take my marbles and go home.

I was a couple of months shy of my 50th birthday and didn't have any idea what I was going to do. I'd been working like a dog since the age of 14. I thought to myself, why not take a little time, smoke some cigars, drink some wine from my cellar, read a bunch of books, and work on my short game. There was plenty of time to sort things out as I enjoyed life outside the office a little.

As I walked out of AT&T Capital that October day, my long-time assistant Jean Watmough helped me carry some of the last boxes, sniffling, with tears in her eyes. With hardly a glance over my shoulder at what I was leaving behind, I threw that collection of stuff accumulated over the years into my Jeep Grand Cherokee and headed straight for the golf course. It was weird.

The last couple of months of negotiating had been very squirrelly. AT&T Capital's CEO Wajnert—my boss and the man who had made my professional life so rewarding and at the same time so maddening for so many years—had cut his own deal, a very sweet deal. Good for him, but some of us were feeling more than a little left out.

*   *   *

My retirement lasted four days.

An executive recruiter called, telling me Compaq was starting its own captive finance company and was searching for a CEO. Would I be interested in coming to interview for it? I had been recommended by a guy I knew at Goldman Sachs, who was consulting for Compaq on the captive finance company project. "Look," I said, "I'm thinking about cigars, good books, my short game. I'll get back to you." As fate would have it, in the fall of 1996, downpours drowned New Jersey as if it was a tropical rain forest. It rained and rained. Then it rained some more. It was the worst autumn anyone could remember in New Jersey. So much for working on my short game.

I flew down to Houston to discuss my future with Compaq's senior management team. The CFO, Earl Mason, and I hit it off like long-lost brothers. We had a lot in common. Earl was from Jersey City, also in Hudson County, just north of my hometown of Bayonne. Like me, Earl had a background at AT&T. We knew a lot of the same people. Instant chemistry. I knew he was my guy, but I didn't necessarily want to move to Houston. On the other hand, I knew this was an opportunity that would be hard to resist.

You have to understand. If God decided to take me at that moment, I would have been okay. I'd taken care of my family. I'd never gotten to number one; I was number two for 11 years. But even as the second in command, I did a lot of great things, helped create a great company. On the other hand, in my last seconds, I'd be thinking how I never got to be number one. The Compaq job was my chance to silence potential regrets.

How this chapter of my career, running Compaq Financial Services, would unfold was unclear at first. Compaq thought they knew what they wanted, but they were thinking small—6, 8, 10 people, selling your receivables to somebody, collecting big forwarding fees. That wasn't my idea of how to make a splash with this new business.

"Earl, that's fine," I said, "You can run it that way if you want, but you are really missing out on a fantastic opportunity."

I hit him with my best shot. There was nothing like actually having a captive finance company, I told him. I reviewed my experience that offering the client the full package—not only products, but an efficient, in-house means of financing—offered an enormous competitive advantage. There were a number of different business models to choose from.

With a company such as Compaq, you want to drive customer behavior and create differentiation in the marketplace. You've got to have a potent sales staff, one that's quick, nimble, and responsive. You've got to have financing products that are aligned with parent company strategies. You want to use financing to control the customer footprint, I continued, rattling off a long list of arguments for going big and the value of doing so.

"That makes a lot of sense. Is this what you did at AT&T?" Earl asked me. Exactly. That was just part of the selling job. They needed to realize they had an enormous opportunity here, the chance to build an aggressive, vibrant financial services company with a billion-dollar-plus upside. It was a lengthy process. I met with everyone that day who mattered, moving from one office to the next. It was a demanding day, and others would follow.

My final meeting, after several weeks had gone by, was with Eckhard Pfeiffer, Compaq's chief executive officer. By the time we got to sit down, I surmised correctly that he was already sold on my hiring and my approach to building this new company. We spent the first part of the interview talking about Porsches, a shared interest.

Then he cut to the chase. "Where do you want to put the company? He asked. "Houston isn't a financial services town." Compaq had gone a long way toward making its mark in a traditional oil town, but Houston was still, well, Houston. Even though the company had done extraordinarily well over the years, Houston wasn't the first place that leapt to mind while assessing the prospects for a global financial services company.

I had my own list of more favorable locations—New York, Boston, and San Francisco, in that order. San Francisco would have been a terrific place for this company—I'd lived there for several years early in my career and absolutely loved the city—but I explained that my best network was in New York and I could assemble a team there fastest. So I said that and oh, by the way, New Jersey is close to New York and . . . "I don't care," Eckhard cut me off. "Just do it."

The challenge was formidable. Eckhard wanted Compaq customer financing to be up and running in the United States, Europe, and Asia Pacific markets, and fast. To me, this process would require considerable, painstaking time and effort if we were going to get it right. Starting a big, complicated global enterprise isn't something you do overnight.

"You know, it will take us two to three years to build an American business, then we can look at Europe, then Asia Pacific," I estimated—quite reasonably, I thought. "The whole thing should take six, maybe seven, years."

"We'd be thinking about months," he said. I took a deep breath. This would be interesting, to say the least.

I flew back to New York. There was one last bit of business to accomplish. I hadn't formally gotten an offer. Earl Mason was going to be in New York the day after my meeting with Eckhard. He wanted to close the deal then, and he planned a nice dinner at the Ritz Carlton on Central Park South to tie up any loose ends.

"Before we order, let's get this out of the way," Earl said, reaching inside his jacket pocket. It was the offer letter. For Earl, my John Hancock was a formality. Not so fast. I wasn't that far removed from thinking my short game would be my daily priority. Everything had to be just right before I took the plunge.

"You know, maybe there are a couple of things we ought to get straightened out first," I said. "I've got a couple of questions."

With that, I leaned over my briefcase and pulled out a yellow legal pad. The pad didn't have just a few notes jotted down, but was filled with questions—about 15 pages worth. Earl looked quizzical.

Question #1: What's the investment hierarchy like at Compaq?

"Any capital expenditure decision above 10 million dollars must go to the board," he said. Before he could continue, I stopped him. "You guys don't want a captive finance company, so you should keep that letter in your pocket."

Let's have a nice dinner, I told him, and we'll go our separate ways.

"Whoa, whaddya mean?" he said.

For Compaq Financial Services to succeed, I said, it had to be authorized to make the big decisions without running everything by the board. The late Speaker of the House Tip O'Neill used to say that all politics is local, and that was the case with a business like ours. I'd say that 85 or 90 percent of this new operation would be local, and then there are the really big deals. We would need agility, speed, and flexibility to develop a deep and dedicated customer base and keep it satisfied if this thing was going to fly.

Say you've got a customer on the books for $8 million in receivables. And the same company wants to do a $5 million deal on top of that. It isn't a $5 million dollar deal—it's a $13 million exposure. When we look at a deal like that, we have to look at the full $13 million exposure. Under those circumstances, had I agreed to Earl's terms, I'd be running back to the Compaq board every time, definitely a customer responsiveness issue. When I was serving as CFO of AT&T Capital, we were always out of compliance with the schedule of authorizations because we were growing so rapidly. That's why I created a "living schedule," one that would automatically adjust as we got bigger. Before that, I figured it was best to act now, and ask for forgiveness later.

"I happen to have a draft schedule of authorizations here," I said, dropping an 80-page document on the table. My briefcase must have weighed 10 pounds that day. "I want you to take this to the Compaq board and have them authorize it."

Two elements were essential to building any successful operating model, and they were not negotiable. The first was establishing a workable governance model that could at once keep the board apprised of decisions and still confer sufficient flexibility to react to the needs of the marketplace and our customer base.

What we had always stressed before and have insisted upon since, which quickly became clear in my dissertation to Earl over dinner, was that a combination of these two vital considerations were critical to future success. He needed a strong governance model *and* a control environment that allowed the chief executive and his leadership team or their designees to be nimble and responsive.

When you run a business, things frequently happen that are completely unforeseen—a deadly and devastating tsunami in Japan in early 2011, the British Petroleum Gulf disaster of the summer of 2010, a litany of shocking product recalls on the scale of the terrible Tylenol poisoning case in the 1980s. Some management teams respond well. Others, as we've seen in far too many cases, do not.

I've always felt that failure to resolve the biggest challenges that you confront—if they are managed poorly or without any evidence of foresight or a mechanism for rapid response—means you're probably not worth the money they're paying you. There is simply no excuse for not having a sound control environment. What you want, of course, is the direct responsibility to respond as quickly and efficiently as possible to the forces of the markets and the needs of the customer. You can't abide a rigid and restrictive environment that impedes your ability to respond. That could leave your business uncompetitive, and lead to your taking that walk to the door at the end of the hall that dumps you onto the sidewalk.

Risk management has never been as important as it is today, as we continue to career from one calamitous global crisis to another. That's why most senior risk management leaders are now seated at the right hand of the CEO; never has their expertise meant more to the survival of the enterprise.

In the risk management hierarchy we've put in place at Hewlett-Packard Financial Services, I can authorize a deal for a considerable amount of money myself without having to extract explicit approval from the Hewlett-Packard board. The HPFS Global Credit Committee's authority is even higher. Our most junior people have authority to handle deals up to $25,000.

And it's not just about credit. You want your employees to be thinking, to be alert. This is a business where fraud gets perpetrated. Our people need to know what the signs are; we train the heck out of them. Even then, from time to time we may run into something that's not kosher, because non-kosher problems can surface.

Our business is evaluating and taking and managing risk. A .300 batting average just doesn't cut it in this business. We're looking for that .980 batting average. So our governance model provides strong guidance for our employees, while encouraging a can-do attitude. Get the deal done—that's of paramount concern—but do it right, don't take any shortcuts.

★   ★   ★

These were some of the points I made to Earl as we discussed our futures over that New York dinner. In moving ahead with the concept of establishing a captive finance operation, Earl and Eckhard were entrusting me to fill the customer financing hole that was somewhat inhibiting their revenue growth. But we had to do it my way before I'd agree to join them.

We would be introducing a whole new concept of a captive finance company inside an information technology company that was already enormously successful. Here you had a guy like Earl Mason who was great with the balance sheet, great with the income statement, great with cash flow, and knew exactly where to find the right managerial levers.

Earl understood that a captive finance company was exactly the right idea for Compaq. He realized they needed to be competitive in the enterprise space. But those same levers that made him such a successful IT financial executive were a bit less effective in captive finance. It was an industry he just didn't know as well as I did.

You can't have a situation where you must get board approval every time there's a deal of $10 million or more. Just won't work. You can have a company structure that you use as a bludgeon, or you can say this is the structure that supports what we're trying to do. It isn't always easy for a truly global enterprise, which Compaq was in the 1990s. From a cultural standpoint, some people in some places around the world are more attuned to a more rigid and structured hierarchical model, and it is more of a challenge to make it work.

In some ways, Goldman Sachs had sold Compaq a bill of goods. They had told the Compaq management team they could hire maybe five or six people, lay the paper off, investors will pay you forwarding fees, and—voilà!—you've got a captive finance business. Certainly, that's one way to go. Apple and Sun Microsystems had gone that route, and it worked for them in a limited way. But as I laid out my vision to Earl that night, I insisted that wasn't a good model for Compaq. You can't do something on that scale half-assed. It has to be an all-or-nothing approach to financing your business; the financing team must be fully on board, dedicated and committed and functioning as part of the Compaq team.

You are not going to get that level of commitment and service from a third party. You're just not going to get the required level of performance. That model was fine for Apple, because it wasn't competing in the enterprise space. My job was to educate Compaq on that and have them buy into the program if this professional marriage was not to be doomed.

★   ★   ★

I wasn't sure how Earl would respond. This was a lot to ask for, in effect telling the Compaq board their policy in this area had to go. "You got it," Earl replied. This might seem like a gutsball move on my part, but it wasn't a bet. I simply wasn't prepared to sign on to something that wasn't designed for success.

We shook hands, I signed Earl's paperwork, and what do you know? I was the new CEO of Compaq Financial Services Corp.

I've thought about what might have happened if November of 1996 had been unseasonably mild, perfect for a daily round of 18 holes. Or if Milton from Goldman Sachs had recommended someone else to the recruiter looking for somebody to run Compaq Financial Services. Or if maybe I'd done a 180 and decided to go in a completely different professional direction. Life would have been quite different.

But I realize now that getting the opportunity to run my own company was something I might never have had the chance to do again. We had built a model to be admired and emulated in the creation of AT&T Capital. And we were able to transport that thinking and innovation to Compaq, and later to Hewlett-Packard Financial Services. We've used that as a foundation to survive—and thrive—during the recessions of the early 1990s and in early 2000–2001, not to mention the Great Recession of 2007–2010.

After Earl grabbed his return flight to Houston, it began to sink in. I had a chance to create something special. I realized that this could assure my legacy as a leader in the industry. I had gotten to the number one position, and that was gratifying. But I had no management team, no assets, no revenues, no specific place to put everybody once we really got the ball rolling. A clean sheet of paper. What, me worry? I realized yet again that you have to be careful what you wish for.

★   ★   ★

So there I was in the early days of 1997 with a new company to run. I had a mandate from the CEO of Compaq to get moving, and quickly. No time to bask in the limelight. What I believed would take years to build—first the American business, then on to Europe and Asia Pacific in sequence—was clearly at odds with what Eckhard Pfeiffer, Compaq's CEO, was expecting.

I started recruiting the rest of the best of the AT&T Capital team. First on board was my good friend and AT&T Capital general counsel Dan McCarthy. It had been a couple of months since AT&T Capital had changed hands.

The company I had helped to lead for more than a decade wasn't the company I had known in the mid-1990s. During the final months, I had found myself falling into periods of disappointment and despair. Once that sale was in the books, my choice was to be gone. Dan and I were the only two of the senior management team who had said "no thanks" to staying even before the ink had dried on the Nomura purchase.

Dan had been with me from the outset at AT&T. He didn't know much about financial services at first. He certainly knew nothing about the leasing business. But he came in eager, a smart guy, Notre Dame Law School graduate and former federal prosecutor. Early on, back in the days of investment tax credit retention deals, we asked him to prepare a lease document for us.

He hired the law firm of Sidley and Austin to assist him. The senior tax partner from Sidley was Bill Golden. Bill was an old pro, very professorial and detail-oriented. Bill and Dan closeted themselves over the course of more than a month in preparation of their tax work, with Dan checking in with me from time to time with updates.

Finally, he walked into my office one day carrying an 85-page document. "This is the greatest lease document in history," Dan declared. "We will never lose in court with this." He was feeling triumphant, quite satisfied with the fruits of his labors. I was about to burst his bubble.

"Dan, you're 100 percent right, because no customer is *ever* going to sign that thing," I said. Abashed by my reaction, they went back to the drawing board and came up with a lease that was more marketable, more customer-friendly. Every chief executive needs a talented legal gunfighter guarding his flank. That man, for me, has been Dan McCarthy. We've known each other more than 25 years, through thick and thin, professional highs and lows.

With Dan on board, I now had to put together a complete senior management team. My old employers, as it happened, unwittingly contributed to my ability to bring in top talent. AT&T had been distracted about things at the end and hadn't forced me to keep my team at arm's length for a prescribed period of time, as most companies do when their top executives leave the business. I had no non-compete, no non-solicit, nothing. They let me walk out the door free and clear, so of course the first thing I did was to try to recruit my old team. Stealing the best and brightest from my former employer was highly satisfying. After all, I had raised many of them from pups.

In early March 1997, I invited Dan to my house in Westfield, New Jersey. Our senior management team was still lean and mean—just Dan and me at that point, although the free agent market was developing, and we were hoping to be active players. But we needed to have a senior staff meeting. It was a miserable, wintry Saturday morning. Dan volunteered to bring the bagels. For the rest of the day, the two of us sat around my kitchen table, talking, laughing, reviewing the papers we scattered round, brainstorming, and taking notes.

It was one of those memorable occasions when ideas were thrown out, debated, and eventually used as pillars of a comprehensive operating plan for a new company. This was where the operating model for Compaq Financial Services was first articulated.

Our meeting that morning would come to be known in company lore as the Kitchen Table Summit—the writing of a statement of principles for our new company and an operational game plan to back it up. We had an excellent precedent for our document, the business model that we'd put in place at AT&T Capital.

I was feeling confident that we were off to a promising start, but I still felt nervous about getting this baby airborne. There was so much at stake. I truly believed this might be a last chance to create a great finance company from the ground up. Such was the magnitude of the opportunity, at least to my way of thinking. Thankfully, Compaq was very supportive. We had given them a business plan that made good sense, incorporating the innovations and strategic positions we'd made a staple during our time at AT&T and molding them to fit the Compaq environment.

When you do anything from a standing start, there can be hiccups, expectations that maybe were a little higher than they should have been. The phone was hardly ringing off the hook at the beginning, but once we got the ball rolling, the ball really got rolling. From mid-year 1998, when momentum really kicked in, until the announcement of the merger in 2001 with Hewlett-Packard, we grew to $3.4 billion in assets and a billion dollars in revenue.

In the earliest days, we hunted office locations and talked about the costs of making Compaq Financial Services a viable business. There was no guarantee how all of this would turn out. I was concerned about expenses. We ended up subleasing space in the old Sunshine Baking Company offices in Woodbridge, a dusky industrial town in central New Jersey intercut by the New Jersey Turnpike and Garden State Parkway, with one warehouse after the next making up its corporate architecture. The Sunshine building was a typical structure for this part of industrial New Jersey, big, sterile, and drafty.

When we first toured the facility, posters and signs depicting the Keebler elves were still hanging on walls and strewn about the place. You remember those elves, of course. They were all the rage at the time in television commercials, cute and cuddly and living in tree hollows, not New Jersey office buildings. But cookies and crackers were part of the building's past. We were going to use it to "manufacture" the best in captive finance; I was sure of that.

The space, about 10,000 square feet, was dirt cheap. It could be our location for a few years, I figured. In the meantime, while they were renovating the space, the building's owners stuck us in temporary quarters on the first floor. "Us," at the start, wasn't exactly a roaming horde of managers, salespersons, and support staff. But we were growing steadily and consistently across the board.

We had folding tables and chairs, telephone cables running across the floor with tape over them. When Gerri Gold came aboard in May of 1997, we were still a small outfit, but planning an expansion. She got something like Badge #8 upon arrival. I put her in a storeroom with boxes piled high. Mind you, Gerri had come from a place where she had two secretaries and custom-made furniture. Here, if you found a bridge chair in your office, you were living the dream.

Gerri Gold had predated me at AT&T Credit Corp., part of the team that was instrumental in persuading me to select Socio-Tech as our operating model. I saw right from the start that she was smart, committed to the business, and driven to succeed. Those are, of course, three attributes that characterize the best of the senior leaders in business, and Gerri had them in abundance. She also brought two critical intangibles to her work—an unassailable work ethic and a magnetic personality.

But even all of those wonderful qualities couldn't guarantee her a reliable phone line in those early Keebler days. Her phone didn't work for three days. Her computer didn't work for a week and a half. When I gave her a list with 20 priorities and said, "I have to have all of this done—like yesterday," she had to be wondering what she had gotten herself into.

She had been an important part of AT&T Capital's growth and success, but it was becoming a place she didn't want to be. She and I had always had a terrific working rapport. Now, after all these years working for me in various positions and companies, she is richly experienced in my ways of doing and thinking about the business. Years later, Jon Flaxman, a colleague of ours at Hewlett-Packard, said about us that at meetings we "finish each other's sentences."

We outgrew the Keebler's space in about 20 minutes. Steadily bringing more people on board, we grabbed every bit of available space we could find. We took away everybody's conference room; we commandeered the kitchen. The only thing left that hadn't been converted to offices or defined workspaces were the bathrooms. That's where we drew the line. I knew that eventually, we'd find ourselves in a position where we'd look back on our Keebler days, and it would seem funny.

We were going to do it all over again—only much better this time.

★   ★   ★

Fast-forward several months. The American business is operational, Europe is moving well along, and we've begun working on the Asia Pacific business. We had accelerated the pace to meet Eckhard's breakneck timetable. I thought it might kill me, but here we were. The top people were in place, and we had a solid plan that would generate business and revenues. Didn't we?

One night that October of 1997, I literally woke up screaming in the middle of the night—we were going about it all wrong. We were building these regions to be separate entities, silos, independent, on their own. We've got something going in Latin America, but they won't be talking to Europe. Asia won't be talking to the United States. I was convinced that our plan—and all the time and expense we'd already poured into it—was a mistake. We were going to screw this up. Our global multinational customers were going to want one deal, consistently delivered and comprehensively deployed around the world—not something lacking alignment and artificially defined by geographic boundaries.

My team just happened to be in town. I called them into a conference room to break the news that everything they knew was wrong, everything they thought they understood and believed about this up-and-coming global enterprise was about to change. Tear up the blueprints and let's go back to the drawing board. I was pretty sure this wouldn't be universally embraced. I wanted to draft one unifying model for doing business in all of our global markets. Some individual fiefdoms, protected and impervious to outside attack, were about to have their flanks exposed.

"Guys, we gotta build one company on a worldwide basis," I began. Some of my team thought it a great idea. The managing directors in charge of Asia Pacific and Europe, needless to say, did not. It was a testy meeting, but when we broke, the locomotive was moving ahead. The naysayers had two choices—get on board the outbound train or stay behind in the station.

Afterwards, there was a little voice in my head saying, "Not so fast." Could we really do this? Should we? This was a dramatic shift in how the company was going to operate on the global stage; it was groundbreaking for the financial services industry. I rarely second-guessed myself, but this decision was preying on my mind. What if I was wrong?

I called Das Narayandas, then an assistant professor at the Harvard Business School. Das was a friend and someone I respected enormously. Today, Das is a full professor and chairman of Harvard's Program for Leadership Development. I asked him if we could get together.

"Booked solid," he replied. To which I responded, "Hell, you've got to eat, right? How about lunch?" Me, the guy who hates lunch. But this was important. "Too busy," he replied. I kept insisting until he finally relented, setting aside an hour.

I flew up to Boston the next day. When we walked out of the Harvard Business School faculty dining room at 5:30 that afternoon—a whole lot longer than the hour that either one of us expected to spend—he was still skeptical that this global model could succeed. Nobody operates on the world stage as one company . . . never been done . . . you're breaking the mold. I took all his counsel and cautions to heart, but ultimately they didn't alter my thinking.

"This will never work," he said before we parted, "but in case it does, take good notes."

It took us years to get this going. You know what it takes to build a backbone system around the world? It is nearly impossible.

Why? Language, currency, legal issues, tax, credit, collections, national accounting rules and regulations—all of the complexity you can possibly imagine trying to do business internationally and yet somehow accommodating it in one consistent system. Whew!

We never discussed it with Eckhard, because I knew it was exactly the right thing to do. As I sat in on his senior leadership meetings, his regional leaders would say something like, "Well that's fine, but you're not doing it in Europe." Yes, we would be doing it in Europe—and everywhere else, for that matter.

After all the back and forth, and putting the plan into practice, it worked. I didn't keep the kind of notes Das suggested I should, but years later he came back and gave a speech to our leadership group and admitted, "I was wrong. You guys have created something unique."

Unique, perhaps. But how could we ensure that this global model would succeed on a global scale? It was time to make our vision a reality.

Chapter 8

One Company, Worldwide

Building a global business isn't an afterthought. I've been doing business internationally since the late 1980s, and, just like everything else in my career, it has been a journey of understanding. The circumstances of global trade and commerce have evolved markedly since my first days at AT&T. But I believe it's actually easier in many ways to operate successfully in the global markets now than it was 25 years ago, even though the world economic stage is far more complicated and competitive.

We live in a world of instant communication. In large part, from a business perspective, everybody around the world wants or needs basically the same things. Sure, there are nuances of difference: language, obviously, as well as tax law, commercial law, and other distinguishing factors. The European Union, for example, has one currency but no unified political structure, no accountability for common objectives. That adds an interesting wrinkle to the equation.

We witnessed that in the often caustic 2010 debate among EU members over how to keep Greece from flying over the cliff. The Germans, for instance, were reluctant at first to spend billions on such a major bailout, given the relatively secure state of their own economy. Clearly, the collective campaign to shore up the Greek economy exposed some of the fraying threads of unity that are bound to persist when many distinct political systems seek to cohere in a singular governing structure. Companies can learn valuable lessons from a dynamic such as this.

So many factors play into deciding how, when, and where to expand your U.S. business internationally. I have a priority list—a core group of global operating guidelines, if you will—that have focused my thinking since I first dove into the global business pool a quarter-century ago.

First, follow the money. When you go global, you've got to follow the money; pick your spots based on customer opportunities. Sounds simple, right? Too many executives deviate from that first essential rule, launching businesses in risky markets without assessing the long-term impact. Their companies are the ones that usually pay the price for shortsighted thinking.

On my second day as head of Compaq Financial Services in 1997, I was in Houston at the company's headquarters, using the visitor's space next to the CEO's office. A phone call came in for me. It was from the country manager for Compaq in Turkey.

"Is this Irv Rothman?" the voice on the other end of the line asked. "This is the country manager for Turkey."

"Well, hello, nice to meet you," I said.

"You must come here immediately," he demanded. So much for the niceties. "If I don't get financing to support my business, I cannot possibly survive. You must come here, and you must come next week."

Now, I would certainly give that leader an A for effort and persistence. But the reality of the moment was something different. Here I was, a CEO with a brand new company, no assets, no sales staff. I had confidence that we would build a strong financing arm for Compaq in due time. But not on the second day. It's fair to say a trip to Turkey wasn't in the cards anytime soon. That was more than 15 years ago, and I think we only got up and running finally in Turkey a few years ago. A very tough road, but one that I saw coming.

Beyond the money, my other rules for building a profitable global business include avoiding countries without something resembling a uniform commercial code or that lack strong banking laws and regulations. Licensing demands must be studied. The type of government in place is critical; dealing with a democratic, free trade–oriented country is far different from trying to swim against the tide of autocratic, even dictatorial regimes. A divisive socio-economic social structure is a definite nonstarter.

Tax breaks, incentives, or other forms of government assistance, while not essential, are always welcome. The depth and breadth of a skilled labor pool, and the cost of hiring, training, and maintaining a workforce are also primary considerations. Understanding the culture of a country, its people, and its business community is of paramount importance. There are a million factors that can make or break a proposed expansion. In some cases, the revenue opportunity isn't substantial enough to over-come the risks. That alone can drop the idea to the bottom of the list.

Even with all of these commercial and cultural variants, I find many more similarities than differences among global customers—either they will buy your value proposition, or they won't, regardless of where you make your case. They expect your products and services to be delivered consistently, efficiently, with minimal fuss, and at a reasonable price.

Operating as "one company worldwide" has been an integral part of my business philosophy since the earliest days. Occasionally, global ambitions can make life tough. Each of our regions has its own set of financial and operating targets to hit annually. Yet to serve our global multinational customers better than our competitors do, we have to be able to transcend geographic boundaries and deploy from a global mindset. Not an easy thing to do with what's going on locally. For a leadership team that is committed to the concept and acting as though they are, staying on message is a must. It's still something we work diligently to perfect at Hewlett-Packard Financial Services, as we did at Compaq before that and at AT&T Capital before that.

Our ability to out execute the other guy in offering a consistently deployed, comprehensively delivered global product has been a market differentiator for us. That must be backed up by a well-developed and thoroughly vetted strategy of expanding to global markets, hiring the best country talent, and capitalizing on economic trends and advantages.

In addition to the United States, we have offices in Dublin, Kuala Lumpur, Shanghai, Mexico City, São Paolo, and many other cities throughout Asia, South America, Europe, and Australia. In selecting potential markets, we've examined a range of options. On the surface, they can seem to be no-brainers. And sometimes they add a more interesting twist.

Take Wroclaw. Wroclaw, where we chose to locate some of our European back-office capabilities, is Poland's fourth-largest city with a population of more than 600,000. It's the capital of a province with nearly 3 million people. The pool of available labor is strong. At first glance, it might not seem a classic location for one of our most important global operations. The city is located in Lower Silesia, closer to Berlin than Warsaw, and benefits from a rail and road infrastructure created during the country's days under German and Austrian rule.

Wroclaw sits alongside the Oder River and has some of the cultural and artistic trappings of other, more famous European cities, with a baroque-style city hall and a 6,000-seat auditorium. The auditorium is listed among the United Nation's World Heritage sites. But the city in particular, and Poland in general, suffered through an extremely challenging period of economic debilitation in recent years.

At its worst, unemployment in Poland has been more than 14 percent; the rate in Wroclaw hovered around 9 percent. Young, skilled workers were fleeing the country for the promise of work and a better life in other European capitals, London in particular. Government figures tell a rather shocking story—more than 400,000 Poles left the country between 2004 and 2008 for Great Britain alone, where jobs and opportunity were far more plentiful.

Yet we saw boundless potential, and we've not wavered in our commitment to the city and to the people of the region. Wroclaw is our second-largest foreign operation, after Dublin. The keys to committing to a place like Wroclaw were an eager and plentiful pool of skilled labor, government incentives, an innovative spirit, and a sense of genuine political stability.

Heirs of a former Communist regime, the Polish government and people have made a remarkable conversion over the past three decades to the principles and practice of capitalism. Most of our people in Poland are young, but they're not babies. Typically, this is not their first job. They are in their mid- to late-twenties, well educated, and well spoken.

They have language skills needed for the rest of Europe—even if you're more likely to find workers who speak Norwegian or

Swedish in Dublin. We applied those principles in selecting Dublin as our primary location for European operations. Hewlett-Packard Financial Services is divided into three regions—the Americas, covering all of North, Central, and South America; EMEA, which oversees our European, Middle Eastern, and African businesses; and Asia-Pacific.

In choosing Dublin, we spent a lot of time thinking through all of the possibilities in 1998, four years before Compaq would become part of the Hewlett-Packard global operation. To me, the Dublin decision made imminent good sense. At the time, the Irish government was offering tremendous tax advantages for multinational companies willing to locate there. At one point, almost every financial services company worth its salt had regional headquarters in Dublin. This is where I wanted Compaq Financial Services to make its European stand.

However, it was anything but an easy sale with the corporate leadership. We had big fights with Compaq over locating in the Irish capital. Compaq's European headquarters were in Germany. They couldn't for the life of them understand why we wouldn't want to establish our regional beachhead there.

Compaq Europe was being run by Andreas Barth. Andreas was an executive with Compaq from 1988 to 1999, first as chief executive in charge of the German business, then as general manager of EMEA from 1991 until he left the company. He was part of the inner circle of Eckhard Pfeiffer, Compaq's CEO, and served as his point man in Europe during the company's meteoric rise in the early- to mid-1990s.

Fortune Magazine, profiling the company in the mid-1990s, described Eckhard's global team as "beefy and intense." Andreas certainly was intense. He was the toughest son of a gun on the planet, a real snake eater. I flew to Germany to discuss with Andreas the thinking behind our choice for a Compaq Financial

Services headquarters in Europe, expecting anything but a welcome embrace of the recommendation.

"You're going to put it in Munich, of course," he said, early in our conversation. "Why is there any discussion?"

My response: "The tax structure, and therefore the profitability structure, is vastly superior in Dublin." Over the course of the meeting, I laid it all out as to why the financial services business would be far better situated from a tax and profit standpoint somewhere other than Germany. My rationale was clear and well-considered, though I figured he would fight me on it.

Andreas couldn't refute the logic. We were going to operate Compaq's European financing operation at a very low marginal composite tax rate—elsewhere, we'd be operating at roughly 30 to 35 percent. This was going to give us a competitive edge in the pricing we'd be able to offer our customers.

"Andreas, not only is the shareholder going to be able to make more money, but I'm going to be able to price skinnier," I assured him. "I'll be able to get my return, and you'll be adding a more competitive financing component to your proposals. The customers will be all over it."

Ireland at the time was aggressively pursuing new business and offering a skilled labor pool in a manner that would be more or less replicated in Poland years later. In terms of tax structure and business growth potential, the Ireland of the late 1970s to the mid-1980s was an unappealing place. Ireland faced an exodus of young talent to countries promoting good jobs and superior career options. It was a classic brain drain, and the country was reeling.

To their credit, Irish government officials realized they needed something to stimulate the Irish economy. That something was companies like ours. They offered tax inducements, and global companies took note and starting opening offices in Dublin. Good jobs followed, and many of those skilled workers who had been quick to leave years earlier began to return.

The comparisons with Wroclaw are striking. Demography, economic conditions, replenishment of the labor pool—all of those factors made a country in severe economic straits a very attractive place to develop a European business. In fact, at one point during a meeting in Wroclaw, I turned to one of our Irish managers who had come along to help with transition and mused, "You know, Poland reminds me so much of Ireland 20 years ago."

"No," he replied, "they're much smarter than we were." He was right; they caught on even faster in Poland. The government wasn't offering the kinds of tax incentives the Irish had granted, but they were offering a much less expensive work force.

You are always examining new, fresh, and potentially lucrative markets. You always wonder, what's the next Dublin? The state of Polish currency could influence future decisions, since the U.S. dollar against the zloty is a pretty good bet at the moment, much better than if Poland were using the euro already. I'm sure we'll continue to have a cadre in Wroclaw for the foreseeable future. When Poland follows much of the rest of Europe and converts to the euro, we'll take another look at it; though, at this point, given the issues currently confronting the European Union, that could take a while. We may go somewhere else, eventually; there is nothing magical about location.

The fundamental question for me is always this: can the company make money in the country? You need to understand all of these ingredients that go into any recipe for success: banking system basics, the presence of something resembling a uniform commercial code, and your ability to integrate and assimilate within the culture.

Does the global economy affect our worldview? Of course, it's a factor. But for us, it's also about where Hewlett-Packard operates.

We've gone through our exploration of the BRIC countries—Brazil, Russia, India, and China. We've established regional headquarters and local offices.

The question for any ambitious, future-directed CEO is what's the next BRIC? What's the next big thing? Deciding how to proceed is an inexact science. In the Compaq days, we bought a company called El Camino. Compaq Financial Services had operations in Mexico, but El Camino had more extensive holdings and promised us a heightened degree of influence not only in Mexico but also throughout South and Central America. The purchase gave us additional business leverage in Argentina, Brazil, Chile, and Peru. Our objective was jump-starting those markets.

As you go global, one question to consider is whether acquisitions are an essential part of growing the business. It certainly is a way to go. In the case of companies like El Camino, they provided the kind of connective tissue you need in countries where the language, culture, and style of doing business make it difficult to establish your own franchise directly. However if you think buying and assimilating a company in the United States is hard, try doing it 3,000 or 4,000 or even 6,000 miles away.

We didn't make many acquisitions, however. The way we generally elected to extend our reach was through joint ventures. Every time we aligned with a company already up and running in our selected market, we negotiated a pre-nup with our new partner, though, because these things almost always go south.

The partner and the captive finance company always have different agendas. We typically had these beauty contests. We would interview four, five, maybe six different prospective business partners abroad, then narrow the candidate list to a final two, perform more due diligence, and seal the deal. It usually was only a matter of time before these agreements started to unravel.

Partnerships gave us scale, allowing us to hit the ground running. And that's precisely what Eckhard Pfeiffer wanted—fast, faster, fastest. I was under orders to take Compaq Financial Services global, and pronto, from the moment I signed on. Not exactly the ideal situation. You can end up fighting all the time when you move so quickly to enlist partners in targeted countries. You have your agenda, and they have their agenda; there's usually some incompatibility between the two sets of interests.

The push/pull exercise is constant. Partnerships are better than nothing, but they're inferior to starting something from scratch with your own agenda, your philosophy, your policies, and your risk-taking practices. Partnership can be a facilitator, a way to get up and running. Of utmost importance is that everything up front is crystal clear—this is who we are, this is what we're doing. Like any marriage between partners of means, you're best advised to negotiate terms of your divorce decree before you take the plunge. It's as though you're saying, "We are entering this exciting new arrangement and we have no doubt it will fail. Please sign on the dotted line. Business is no place for romance. Have a nice day."

When we entered into a joint venture partnership in Asia, Europe, or the Middle East, we'd say, "Okay, here's the deal. This is what the divorce will look like, because there will be a divorce. It may be this year, next year, three years from now. But there will be a divorce." I remember when we severed our relationship with one of our partners in EMEA. I called and said "I think we need to take this to a significantly higher level. Remember paragraphs X, Y, and Z? We're going to execute our 'out.' Thanks for all your help, see you later."

With the global partnership, it's just a matter of expediency. For the partner, it's a nice piece of business. For the captive, it can be nothing less than life or death, and how you're doing on behalf of the parent company. If your partner isn't being aggressive enough or is unwilling to commit the effort and resources required to build a successful joint venture, you're going to have tension. You need to recognize that going in. Your partner may have five or six business relationships, and you're just another spoke in that wheel.

In terms of where you operate, ask yourself: Where is my opportunity? What is my total addressable market? What resources will it take to roll out? How long do I have to wait for a positive return? You have to go through all levels of decision. I've had too many colleagues in the industry over the years who think the idea of going global is great. "We can start it up in England or Germany or France," they figure. "Hey, we can go to Europe a couple of times a year! That sounds like fun. Great food, great sights. Big opportunity."

Big mistake. They too often start from scratch with no customer relationships in their new foreign location. These guys are going in there, renting space for $200 a square foot. They hang out a shingle. In the leasing business, revenue is recognized over the life of the financing term, and you don't make money the first couple of years after you put a deal on the books. It's all expense. In places like England, it's really expensive.

It comes down to this. You have to pay the light bill. A lot of companies set up shop, keep it going for a couple of years without that kind of financial support or preparation. Dinners in expensive European capitals are always nice. But you have to be really smart about the value of locating in a particular place.

You can always throw up that shingle, but if people don't know who you are, you're in trouble. By the time my colleagues decided to expand their businesses globally, they we already well down the road to being successful U.S. companies and were enjoying their success. Maybe a little bit too much, so they forgot what it takes to get to the top of the mountain.

If I were starting a new business today, I'd go to my biggest international customers and say, "Listen, if you like what I'm doing for you here, think what I can do for you worldwide. So let's cut a global deal." That's what I would do to set up a global operation. My partners and customers want and need the support we can provide in their foreign markets. And I want a steady revenue stream. That's the basis of beautiful friendship.

Chapter 9

Global Recessions:
A Survivor's Manual

O ver my career, I've endured recessions of varying size, depth, and duration. Three of those recessions—in the early 1990s, at the start of the new century, and this most recent Great Recession, so debilitating on a worldwide scale—found me in key senior leadership roles, the last two as chief executive officer of a good-sized U.S. based company.

There is no executive education quite like managing through a recession. Nothing tests your leadership ability more, or your skill in juggling the myriad demands of your company, customers, and employees. There are no absolute guarantees that any business, no matter how well-managed, can emerge from a near-depression fully intact. Many will sputter and die.

But, if you manage your business intelligently, through clear eyes and guided by a judicious, analytical sense of mission, the damage of any recession can be lessened. Our most recent economic meltdown was much deeper and more pronounced than anything else I'd seen in my career.

But I think HPFS was in a stronger position during the most recent recession than other businesses, inside and outside our industry, not only to withstand these economic gales, but to actually grow the business. We became more profitable at a time when many of our competitors suffered significant losses. We did so by sticking to a game plan created to maintain steady progress.

In effect, we were better prepared because of everything we did before the recession arrived, not just because of how we reacted once it had gathered momentum. I'd say it starts with a basic philosophy—do what you're good at doing. Too many companies decide to branch out in directions and down paths that are all too likely to lead them to disastrous results.

When some stumbled through recessions, frequently it was because they veered from the core businesses that made them so successful in the first place. Too often, an executive wakes up in the morning and decides, "The business isn't any good anymore; let's start a new one." Business cycles are a reality. Companies improve, they devolve, they change fundamentally over time. As a corporate leader, you have to adjust.

For better than a quarter century, Comdisco was the leading player in the computer leasing industry. That's actually a gross understatement: It was the glamour puss of a business few knew or cared that much about, yet it gained iconic status as a high flying publicly traded company with a somewhat notorious corporate culture. Its founder and CEO, Ken Pontikes, was a legendary figure for both his business acumen and flamboyant lifestyle.

But if there was ever a poster child for a company straying from what had made it so remarkably successful to reach a disastrous end, it was Comdisco. Following Ken's untimely death, his successor decided that the business that had yielded such fantastic results and wealth for shareowners and employees alike was no longer viable. Rather, it was the promise of dot-com riches that became the focus of the company's direction and resources.

Venture capital, telecom, Internet, network . . . Comdisco made investment bets across the board. And, what's more, supported them with a bloated expense and executive structure. When the bubble burst, it all came crashing down. None of the bets paid off, and Comdisco filed for bankruptcy in 2001.

The underpinnings of any successful enterprise are what account for its viability and strength. It's a big world out there. A lot more opportunity exists during a recessionary period than you might think. At HP Financial Services, we've been particularly good at functioning in the enterprise space. We never held a particular funding advantage other than that we had our parent company's balance sheet. Although some of our competitors didn't have that, many did.

That doesn't diminish the need to think long and hard about what we bring to the table when we talk to a customer. Those metrics don't change. What's the real value proposition? How do we make our product attractive to customers? How do we make it a point of differentiation in the marketplace? How do we convince and train the sales staff to sell it?

Those are just a few of the questions that drive strategy generally, but more so in an economic downturn. There's only so much of an expense envelope. Nobody possesses a commanding share of the market, and there is a potentially huge pot of business out there—even in times that are sluggish or worse.

You maintain your equilibrium during down economic times by conducting business with companies that are more creditworthy. That served us especially well during the late 1990s and the explosion of the dot-coms. We had a set of reliable credit-granting philosophies and processes. While not deliberately designed to be recession-proof, they nevertheless served us well when market value fell, businesses contracted, and workers were released.

In this particular recession, we were far better prepared for it than at any other place I'd been. In the early 1990s, when the economy went south, we weren't ready. I was running the redefined AT&T Credit Corp. Half our customer base was small- and medium-sized businesses, or the SMB space. We were making money hand over fist. That part of the business was throwing off 35 percent ROE at 6:1 leverage. And then the spaghetti hit the fan. We'd been working from established formulas that projected accounts receivable over different durations.

When you are talking about small businesses and operating in the SMB space, as we were doing, it's all about overhead expenses: the cost of operating a factory, for example, and controlling credit losses. Often in bad times, customers are calculating how much they can reasonably stretch the payment schedule.

Unfortunately for us, the accounts receivable percentages grew rapidly. It all happened over a very short period. The ditch got deeper, our losses shot higher. Today, you're talking about information technology, but then telephone systems still ruled the roost. You couldn't run a business without a telephone, much as today it's not possible without an adequate IT structure. In both cases, you're talking about essential-use equipment.

In that era, if a business were to survive, they had to have a telephone. Nevertheless, accounts receivable were running 60, 90 days—even 180 days, based on our algorithms, we should have had a better handle on what the losses would look like. Yet we failed to anticipate the depth, severity, and accelerated pace of the losses. It took us several quarters to return to where we needed to be.

This is what so damaged the banking system during the recent economic crisis. Their operating models failed because they weren't making good credit or documentation decisions from the outset. It's crucial, even at time of high profitability, that businesses not be chasing bad deals. In fact, that's when the smartest leaders should be exercising even greater caution and introspection. In a severe recession, the small guys normally get hurt first and most.

I had learned an invaluable lesson from that earlier time. We were invested heavily in the SMB space because it was so profitable. AT&T Capital lost sight of its responsibility to manage carefully, even when there was pressure to loosen the reins. It wasn't so much that our credit-granting processes were out of whack, it was what we didn't do after the deals went on the books. We didn't execute, and so we got our butts kicked. It was our own fault. It's good to eat ice cream, but every now and then, you have to eat some spinach, too. We weren't eating enough spinach.

That period was instructive for all of us. We had the AT&T balance sheet; we took a look at our credit-scoring models and our credit-granting procedures; we examined our collection and recovery procedures. We turned a bright spotlight on the problem and determined that we were going to rectify it. True, we came out of it with scars, but fewer scars, I'd wager, than were suffered at other prominent companies, both in and outside our industry.

That was 20 years ago, more than a generation in business years. I'm a way smarter guy now than I was 20 years ago. At the time, we were focused more on growing the business than on running the business. That's an important distinction, and one that none of us thought about making as the money poured in and our revenues kept rising. Today, I'm focused like a laser on both growing and running the business. That comes with the territory; you have to balance proactive and reactive thinking.

In the midst of this unraveling in the early 1990s, we held one of our periodic senior leadership meetings. Everybody had to discuss how their businesses were doing. I called Tom Wajnert beforehand and asked if we could get together for a cup of coffee.

"Tom," I said, "I'm going to miss my business plan. My losses are going to be deeper than I forecast."

Absorbing losses in excess of what you project isn't exactly part of the plan. But it's worse to walk into the lion's den without some kind of considered, restorative plan. Once in the hole, you need to let people know how you are going to climb out by offering a game plan for what needs to be done on a go-forward basis. I came prepared with a plan.

"We should have handled this better, anticipated this better," I later told the group. "We didn't do that, but we are going to fix it. In the meantime, we're going to have to incur some short-term pain."

Now, some executives are loathe to step up and say, "It's not my fault; the dog ate my homework"; or offer any other excuse. I've never been a dog-ate-my-homework kind of guy. I've always been more buck-stops-here. Leadership isn't about buck-passing, particularly in times of strife for the business and, more broadly, across the economy at large.

One thing that always must be top of mind: Make sure that even in the best of times, you have a team that you sincerely believe possesses the skill levels that will steer you through the *worst* of times. The proof of quality management is not how you perform when the company or market is going great guns. It's how you perform when it isn't.

I remember doing an interview with an industry publication reporter who asked me what worried me the most about running a business. "An economic boom," I said. "When the boom stops, as it inevitably will, are our credit-collection people going to be skilled enough or experienced enough to handle workouts and recoveries, and complete all the tasks that must be completed to keep the business running effectively?"

That's hard to do. But you can ease that by understanding that there will be ups and downs. We're never going to get as rich in the up periods, but we're never going to be hit as hard in the down periods as some of our competitors. I genuinely believe that.

I had the following exchange with Mark Hurd, the former CEO of Hewlett-Packard. "When was the last time you saw HP Financial Services in the *Wall Street Journal*?" I asked him one day. His response: "I've never seen your name in the *Journal*." To me, that's an accomplishment. Never get in trouble, never drive off a cliff, and you won't be news—at least in ways that can hurt the company.

The lessons I took with me from my days at AT&T served me well a few years later when I was named the CEO of Compaq Financial Services, in 1996. I had a clean sheet of paper. We were going to be a player in the enterprise space. We were not going to be a player in the SMB space. That wasn't us. Enterprise was where we needed to be; it was what we did best.

★   ★   ★

My turn in the CEO's chair at Compaq Financial Services coincided with the dot-com boom. Businesses with enormous stores of cash accrued through venture capital investment or IPOs were flooding our radar screens. These were very attractive to many executives. My inclination, however, was to take a step back, assess this unpredictable new wave, and think hard about what it would mean to us and how much of a plunge we should take. Of course, I saw the enormous potential of the Internet as a driver of new, exciting, and perhaps—one day—profitable enterprises.

At the end of the day, we came out all right on the other side of the dot-com bubble. Why? Because as a rule, we didn't do much business with dot-coms. Yes, there were shooting stars among the Internet start-ups, and we were being pressured by the sales leadership to think about cutting deals with these new businesses. But I couldn't go around financing air.

We were cognizant throughout, as we are to this day, of our fiduciary duty to shareholders. Our objective is to deal with the adults, first in the age of Internet start-ups and more recently with social networking and related businesses. In considering a financing arrangement, we have to be practical.

That world had the feel of a digital Wild West. Nothing was assured, and things could turn on a dime. I wasn't averse to financing some of these new businesses if I thought they had credible backing, but even that wasn't always enough. In one instance, we financed an online toy store. The primary investor was a major entertainment company with a very successful track record. We thought if they were the primary investor, this was probably one where we could stick our neck out.

So we did. A year later, the investor pulled the plug. The toy store's performance was from hunger. They were in deep yogurt from the start. Even though that venture, supported as it was by the acknowledged leader in family entertainment, failed, it left an impression with me. When it's a company that is established and indisputably successful, you take the calculated risk. You don't take a shot with a couple of guys who dropped out of Harvard one afternoon with a kernel of an idea, raised millions of dollars on the flimsiest of business plans, and ended up playing ping pong all day long and frittering away their investment capital.

With the advent of social media and the new round of Internet start-ups, some of those same considerations and challenges have returned. The key today, as it was then, is to go as deep as possible when weighing an investment. Sometimes you get a company in the first round of venture capital, sometimes the company is in the fourth round of venture capital. Are these blind faith investments that will do little to keep the business going after six months?

We look at all of those factors—then, now, in the future—when determining whether this is something we want to pursue. Who's investing, what's the management team and the level of its experience, what is their track record of building and sustaining successful businesses? You can't go all in if your players don't have the cards.

Of course, some of those schemes worked out well. Facebook has written quite a success story. Napster, too. But for every one of those ideas that gains flight elevation over time, there are a bunch that crash and burn. I never liked those odds. Still don't. That goes back to the steady hand in managing risk. Credit losses are part of the business. We all understand that, but they have to occur within an acceptable range. If you take no credit losses, you aren't assuming enough risk. Too many, as we've seen all too often over the past decade, and your business could be a fleeting memory.

★   ★   ★

We were feeling the pressure of the dot-com boom and trying to figure out this new market when Eckhard Pfeiffer, the Compaq CEO who hired me to run his financial services businesses originally, was forced out his job in 1999. Michael Capellas replaced Eckhard. Capellas had joined Compaq in 1998 as chief information officer, and now he was running the show. I needed to convince him our operating plan was the right one. I believe in managing up to avoid getting managed down. I knew more about our business than anyone else at Compaq, so my message was clear. We needed to do it our way.

After an interregnum of more than six months, Capellas named an interim CFO, Ben Wells. Ben had been with Compaq since the mid-1980s, and was treasurer during Eckhard's regime. We had always maintained a good working rapport, and he had an excellent grasp of our business and its complications. But Capellas eventually hired a permanent CFO, Jesse Greene, who had a long history at IBM and Kodak. That didn't work out as well.

We were growing very nicely in the market during the last days of the last century, even without the bull's rush into dot-coms. We didn't have to do that business. Look at all of the banking firms making money from derivatives over the past decade. It's not real. Eventually the chickens come home to roost. As Charles Munger, the longtime business partner of Warren Buffett, so aptly put it: "to say that derivative accounting is a sewer is an insult to sewage."

That's how I felt about it then, and that's how I feel about it now. But it's back. Not the first steps of the dot-com advance, but the explosion of social networking sites. Some will succeed; many more will not. It's still a huge risk for a business such as ours to be taking a financial stake in these businesses. Risk taking is an important part of the job description. It's okay to be wrong; it's just not okay to be wrong for the wrong reasons. That is never more critical than during a down economy.

Recently, a sizable deal in Asia Pacific went bad on us. Fortunately, we did so well during our 2010 fiscal year that we covered it, and eventually we should manage to recover a significant percent above our planned losses. But a post mortem was needed to determine what had happened and whether this deal could have been avoided. What did we miss? Did we fail in our due diligence?

We gathered the Credit Committee around the table, and I asked them to present the deal to me exactly the same way they pitched this business the first time around. Basically, I wanted to make sure we weren't asleep at the switch when we signed off on this transaction.

They re-presented the deal—the pros, cons, upside, reasons to move ahead with it all over again if given the option. And we unanimously agreed, again, that it was a deal well worth doing. It had been an existing customer of HP; there was an established track record. Their business was going through a rough patch, we were all aware of it, but they'd been with us for nine years and always exhibited resiliency and an ability to operate through difficult times. In the end, the forces of the recession this time were too crippling, and they succumbed.

There are no guarantees in our business. Even what seem like rock-solid enterprises can suddenly fall off the face of the earth. Sure, it's easy enough to see how some companies find themselves in a fix. All these guys who sold home mortgages to people without getting any financials, without getting pay stubs, without realizing these loans were a complete crapshoot, they were doomed to failure. If you have reliable credit-granting procedures, the odds of deflecting bad deals increase dramatically. You can be wrong for the right reasons.

Deals don't disappear when the economy is tight. They didn't in the early 1990s or at the start of the first decade in the post–9/11 era. They certainly may have been harder to find and book in our most recent conflagration, but they were still out there. In the midst of the recession, I was standing on line in the cafeteria of our New Jersey headquarters next to Fernando Gomez, one of our senior credit managers. We struck up a conversation, and he told me we were still approving a lot of deals—"It's just taking us a little longer to get there." The business is out there, but as Fernando noted, it's taking us a little longer to get to the point where we can push the button.

In the early part of the last decade, when the merger of Hewlett-Packard and Compaq was finalized and we could get rolling on new business, we were presented with an opportunity to finance a Brazilian telecommunications company. They had come to us when I was at Compaq; we turned them down for $50,000. We'd done our due diligence and just thought it prudent to pass. Not Hewlett-Packard Technology Finance (our counterpart at HP premerger). They already had a deal with the company on the books for a half million dollars.

After we finalized the merger in 2002, I asked the people who had been at HP Technology Finance to find out why something we thought so ill advised had looked so good to them. Turns out the telecom had received a visit from an HP senior executive who was impressed by their operation—never mind that they had no creditworthiness to speak of. Not a lot of research had been performed before an agreement was signed. That was an example of a deal done for the wrong reasons. Avoiding a bad decision based on bad reasoning is Financing 101. You can't run a business like that.

This most recent recession was longer, deeper, and far more challenging than any that had come before it, at least in my experience. Companies across the spectrum were forced to cut back. You'd find some surprises, some businesses willing to push ahead aggressively despite circumstances. But they were few and far between. The vast majority retreated to a kind of bunker mentality. Delay, if not fully deny, any and all opportunities. That became the working philosophy. Uncertainty about the next few years continues, with businesses sitting on an estimated $1 trillion or more that they are reluctant to spend.

From our perspective, we managed to navigate the latest downturn more smoothly than most. That doesn't mean we sailed through it without the boat rocking occasionally. In early 2009, spreads were completely insane. The cost of money went through the roof. Our margins were under heavy pressure. How long was this going to last? Our momentum was so strong, and factors well beyond our control were threatening it. How were we going react?

In times of recession, the job becomes exponentially harder. So stick to the basics. Do what you do. Any movement away from the essential business is too risky.

Chapter 10

We're Gonna Go for What's Behind Door Number Three

There's nothing simple about running a business, whether an established enterprise or a new venture, with all of the special challenges that it entails. The most basic advice any senior executive can assimilate is this: "You're the leader, so lead. You didn't wind up in the corner office by accident." Among the many reasons an executive reaches the top is an ability to deal not only with issues that are quantitative and easily identifiable, but also those that are qualitative and intangible.

You need to size up these situations, assessing all relevant factors, and make the call. And you need to do so with conviction, inspiring those around you to go forward and execute with confidence. I like to think of myself as someone who can be per-suaded by a good argument, but reams of data won't persuade me to follow a specific course of action if it doesn't feel right.

A chief executive inevitably must face a myriad of tough deci-sions over the course of a professional lifetime. Our choices can affect thousands, even tens of thousands of employees, and billions of dollars in assets and revenues, for good or bad. In some cases, our choices will determine whether a business succeeds or dies. And not all of these decisions have to do strictly with numbers, analytical projections, or facts that seem to steer the process in one direction or another.

In short, a good leader must deal effectively with ambiguity. It would be nice if the world lined up straight from Point A to Point B. That just doesn't happen in the real world. There are a million different dynamics, and you are going to be faced with ambiguity on a regular basis. Risk versus calculation—how do you chart the best path toward a successful result? First, you can't be afraid. I've never been afraid of the consequences of the decisions I've made.

I've run Compaq Financial Services and, for over a decade, Hewlett-Packard Financial Services. The decisions I've made have had a direct and lasting impact on the lives of those who call HPFS their professional home. I've always believed that the key guiding characteristics are doing the right thing, using sound judgment, following instinct tempered by experience, relying on a strategic foundation, and negotiating effectively once you've chosen your path, no matter how uncertain.

Informed, data-based decision making is ideal. But there's no such thing as foolproof decision making. If there were, stock prices would never drop, the Yankees would be World Series winners every year, and the world just might stop spinning on its axis. Data are always subject to interpretation: bringing the "J" word into the mix is essential. Judgment is rooted not only in cold facts but also in the human factor. From a leadership standpoint, that's where the rubber meets the road. I'd throw instinct into the mix as well—how does it feel? What does your gut tell you? Wins and losses, success and failures, often result from decisions that need to be made in real time, without the benefit of study teams or task forces.

Sometimes the numbers don't stack up, but I've got an instinctive feeling about what will work and what won't. Sometimes you don't have the luxury of ready data. You're not always in control of the timetable. Sometimes opportunities present themselves, and you've got to act on them. And data doesn't always give you everything you need. When people come to me, I ask them for the worst case, what's the downside, how much will we lose if things don't go our way? Is it affordable, does it take our business in the right direction?

You're doing all that stuff in your head when you've got 10 people arranged around the conference table, with charts and graphs lighting up the screen distilling the best thinking and logic they can bring to the issue. One of the things I do is put everyone to the test: How good are your assumptions? How did you reach those conclusions? At the end of the day, it's always a question of what you think of the data, but the data aren't always perfect. You have to understand the market circumstance, your opportunity, your opinion of the potential downside. You've got to make those calls you are paid to make.

It was the end of 1999, into the early days of 2000, and Dan McCarthy and I were in the midst of divorcing our joint venture partners in Europe. They were based in London, and they were doing a terrible job for us. They weren't engaged, pure and simple. It was a nice piece of business for them, but they never committed to it the way they had promised. When you negotiate the terms of a business divorce with a joint venture partner before the ink's even dry on the marriage license, it's a tacit understanding that each side has a different agenda and maybe incompatible long-term goals.

So we had our pre-nup. In this particular case, we were pulling the ripcord fairly early on, the other side was pressing us for more in the way of a financial settlement and presented all of these arguments they felt made sense and were beneficial to them. Dan thought some of their ideas were valid, and he was leaning in the direction of settling the dispute. One day, I walked into Dan's office down the hall, put my feet up on his desk, and said, "Offer them nothing."

"What do you mean?"

"Offer them nothing," I said again. "They are going to go for the deal that's on the table. We need to play a little gutsball with them. Offer them nothing, and that will be what they go for." I was right. They wanted something beyond what was in the pre-nup. They pressed their case, and admittedly their arguments weren't half bad. But I didn't want to give them a nickel beyond the contractual terms.

The whole process took only a couple of days. Dan was quite unhappy with me. I told him, "You're entitled to be unhappy, but this is the way we're gonna do it." It wasn't an astronomical amount of money we were talking about—bigger than a bread-basket, but not significant, either. In the early days of Compaq Financial Services, however, every dollar mattered. In those days, if you wanted 45 cents, I'd fight you tooth and nail.

We were still a comparatively new company, no longer techni-cally a start-up in the sense that we were scrambling for resources and scratching and clawing for basic market share. I needed to be far more cognizant of my bottom line and how any of these global decisions would affect it. I was unwilling to concede an inch. In the face of potential difficulty, we won this particular battle.

★　　★　　★

Balancing risk and reward is always the game plan, but sometimes you have to take your shot. The sun will still come up in the morning. In January 1998, Compaq Computer Corp. announced it had bought Digital Equipment Corp. for $9.6 billion. At the time, it was the largest merger in the history of the computer business. Eckhard Pfeiffer and his management group were in an especially acquisitive mode during the 1990s, focusing on the enterprise market and already the proud owner of several other large computer vendors.

Compaq was becoming an 800-pound gorilla in the personal computer business; the DEC deal made Compaq the number two computer company in the world. Bringing DEC into the fold would also have significant ramifications for Compaq Financial Services—and for me, although I had no idea at the time how big.

DEC had been using GE to handle its financing in the United States, and the GE overseers went to their executive sponsor at DEC, John Randall. They told John they wanted to get to know Compaq, citing the relationship with the DEC portfolio. What's more, they wanted Compaq to name GE as its worldwide outsourcing partner for customer financing, and to sell them the nascent Compaq Financial Services.

"If Compaq doesn't want to do that, they can just buy us out," was the message delivered to Randall.

Being a good guy, Randall picked up the phone and called me in New Jersey. I didn't know him very well, had only met him briefly, but he thought I should be aware of what was happening. He relayed details of the conversation to me and I thought, here we go again. It's not even two years. I can go back to smoking cigars, working on my short game.

But I was invested in this new company, obligated to my team, and not ready to consider retirement again. I called Earl Mason, the CFO of Compaq. Earl and I had hit it off immediately during my courtship by Compaq in 1996, and I could be blunt with him.

"Well, what do you want to do?" Earl asked me.

"I think we should buy those assholes out," I said.

The next day, I put a call in to Steve Bennett, who was the other half of that first discussion with Randall. Typical GE guy—no nonsense, tough talking. I told him I had talked to the Compaq head office in Houston, summarized the content of the conversation, and said that they had authorized me to make this call.

"What do you want to do?" Bennett asked

"We're gonna go for what's behind door number three," I said.

"What?"

"We want to buy *you* out," I continued. Dead silence on the other end of the line. I think he was stunned.

"Does that mean you want the asset management business, too?" Bennett inquired. Something in his voice indicated to me that this was a unit he was reluctant to part with, though I wasn't sure why. He's reluctant; that's good enough for me. He clearly would have liked to exclude that unit from the deal, but if he was being honest, he just didn't feel that he could, and I didn't get the sense he was trying to snooker me. His response was too spontaneous.

All this went through my head in a split second, so, without hesitation, I chimed in, "You bet your sweet ass we do!"

After a short pause, Bennett said, "Okay, we'll get the lawyers working on it."

With that, the conversation ended. We hung up the phones. My next conversation, however brief, was with myself.

"What the hell did you just do? Holy s—!" Here I was, about to be on the hook for an asset management business, in addition to all of the rest of it. The total deal was worth $400 million. At the same time, I also was in the process of buying out DEC's joint venture partner in Europe, De Lage Landen, for another $100 million.

I would in effect be urging the directors of Compaq to give me nearly a half billion dollars to be the financial services arm of DEC, in combination with what we were already feverishly building. The truth of the matter was that I had never been so nervous in my life as at the thought of having to make my case to the Compaq board of directors. I had nothing, really, in the way of assets—about $100 million at the time—and correspondingly little in the way of revenues. We hadn't achieved that strong momentum yet. We were almost a brand-new company.

Sure, we were on plan and doing what we said we were going to do. But you don't go and ask the board of the second-biggest computer company in the world if they'll hand over $500 million to a largely untested, if not unknown, subsidiary management team. Talk about playing gutsball! I was depending on Earl and Eckhard to help me sell this.

To be honest, I didn't want to take on Ben Rosen all by myself. The chairman of the board, Rosen was and is a legendary figure in the computer industry and a renowned venture capitalist, the co-founder of Sevin Rosen Funds. He had a keen eye for new tech companies with lots of upside, as evidenced by his early financial support of Compaq and the software maker Lotus Development Corp.

Though seen as a technology evangelist and industry cheerleader, he could also be tough and unrelenting when it came to CEOs. After Compaq suffered a downturn in 1991, he shocked the computer industry by firing then-CEO—and Compaq co-founder—Rod Canion. That move set the industry back on its heels. By the time I appeared before the board to make my pitch, Rosen was an older, crusty guy, having already served as the most vocal and influential member of the Compaq board for 16 years. I had to bring my A-game, or this very expensive deal could very well blow up in my face.

I flew down to Houston and made my pitch. We had to consolidate, I argued. We can't have all these other companies
representing Compaq and doing customer financing. It made no
sense to be competing against ourselves in the marketplace. You
want to have a consistently deployed operation; you want to
have one face to the market. I was pretty insistent, giving them a
comprehensive financial presentation on how we would make all
this work.

In the end, Rosen gave me a thumbs-up. "Do what you've
gotta do," he said. Later, I tried to figure out why I was so
nervous about the presentation. I really felt I personally had
nothing to lose but I was invested in it, had others counting
on me, and was trying to grow the business. We were small and
finding our way, but I was convinced we had enormous growth
potential.

The asset-management group that was included in the transaction, located in Andover, Massachusetts, became a valuable part of
Compaq Financial Services. From a somewhat impulsive moment
on the phone with a guy from GE, it quickly became apparent
how important a viable asset-management capability would be for
providing a market-differentiating value proposition. This business
is about evaluating, taking, and managing risk. I think I have a
pretty good track record when it comes to weighing the pros
and cons of any deal. You don't always have the advantage of
data-based decisions. Sometimes things just appeal to you at a
certain level.

The grilled cheese lunch all those years before with Paul
Gustavson, that was gut instinct. Absolutely. One company on a
worldwide basis—I just knew that was right. Doing a sharp 180°
turn on our business model less than a year into my tenure at
Compaq—the same thing. You can't be afraid to fail. I feel like
I'm going to make more right decisions than wrong; if I don't, I
won't be long in the CEO's chair.

We're Gonna Go for What's Behind Door Number Three

I was one CEO who escaped the wrath of Ben Rosen. Eckhard wasn't so lucky, and neither was Earl. They would be gone a year later, the victims of a performance stumble—and dispatched by Rosen, who temporarily took the management reins of Compaq while the search for a new permanent CEO was under way.

Chapter 11

Around the World
in 180 Days

The merger of Hewlett-Packard and Compaq, announced just days before the horrific events of 9/11 in 2001, hit The Street like a ton of bricks. Analysts hated the deal. It was excoriated by those supposedly in the know in the financial community. I remember Scott McNeeley, then CEO of Sun Microsystems, disparaging the merger as "two garbage trucks crashing together."

For the company, global terror and its consequences relegated most of our merger news, negative or otherwise, to the inside pages. Years later, most dispassionate observers would probably concede that the deal, however controversial initially, had served Hewlett-Packard well.

Championed by then-CEO Carly Fiorina and supported by a majority of the HP board (director Walter Hewlett, son of the co-founder, being one vocal and persistent exception), the deal combined two major tech enterprises into one. It created a global technology leader, with the industry's most complete set of IT services and products for consumers and businesses alike. We were going to be number one globally in services, access devices, and imaging and printing products, and in the upper tier in storage and management software. The new company was expected to generate revenues of about $87 billion.

As with any merger or acquisition, in a down economy particularly, there were casualties. Starting late in 2000, you couldn't go even a couple of days without an announcement from one tech company or another of massive layoffs and plans to constrict or consolidate the business. The NASDAQ hit an all-time high of 5,048 on March 10, 2000. After that, it was a fast ride downhill.

Our merger was emblematic of the time. Both HP and Compaq employees lost their jobs or saw their positions eliminated because of duplication, consolidation, contraction, or loss of product/service lines between the September 2001 announcement and the formal takeover the following May. Fiorina would be CEO of the combined company, with Compaq's CEO Mike Capellas staying on as COO (the over/under for his tenure was six months, which turned out to be prophetic). Robert "Bob" Wayman, the HP CFO, would remain as the merged company's chief financial officer; our paths would cross very soon.

There was little doubt that my professional life was about to change dramatically. Here I was, someone who had created a new company—Compaq Financial Services—from a clean sheet of paper and steered it through those fledgling days of card tables and lousy phone service at the old Keebler offices in Jersey, watching it grow into a successful financial services company with a bright future.

But Compaq, a galloping racehorse of a company in the early 1990s, had slowed to a trot. The ever-shifting tectonic plates of the computer hardware and software firmament had thrown the company off balance. One way or another, I would come through it all right. I had two options: take a sizable buyout and bid everyone adieu, or accept a retention bonus and the opportunity to remain as part of the new Hewlett-Packard.

HP had launched Hewlett-Packard Technology Finance in 1982. The merger less than two decades later meant that something would have to give. You can't have two captive finance companies serving one parent company. Compaq Financial Services was doing just fine. Our operating system, polished and improved since those early days at AT&T Capital, served as a steady source of revenue-generation and customer satisfaction for the company.

Soon after news of the merger was released, I was summoned to HP's headquarters in Palo Alto, California, to talk to Wayman. I was a senior guy at Compaq, but had no clue what HP wanted from the customer financing side. I figured I had nothing to lose, so I put my cards on the table. I told Wayman the HP Tech Finance business was, to my way of thinking, lacking. It had operated from three or four different business models in the preceding five years, with four or five different leaders overseeing the business, some of them dispatched from the HP Controller's office to oversee this somewhat neglected division.

By comparison, I continued, Compaq Financial Services was successful because it benefited from experienced leadership, a strong business foundation, one that held people accountable and gave them the kind of buy-in that raised productivity and morale and served the customer well. We spoke a little about the operating model that had become the basis of my management philosophy.

We shook hands. I left. It took me back to that conversation years ago with Earl Mason, the CFO of Compaq, and our dinner in New York during which I laid out my business philosophy— and my terms for coming on board as the first CEO of Compaq Financial Services. I had supreme confidence in our operating model; after all, it had twice proven to be successful.

In the aftermath of the Wayman meeting, I was of two minds. In a way, I didn't really care whether I would be running the captive finance business eventually. I was going to get the same amount of money regardless. But of course, it did matter to me. This was my team, a business I had built, where I had invested untold energy and commitment.

It was 2001, I was almost 55 years old, and life was good financially. I had no thoughts of retiring, however. Was I genuinely interested in leading the new Hewlett-Packard Financial Services? If the circumstances were right, sure. But everything had to align.

A couple of weeks later, Wayman called. He wanted me to lead the combined HP customer financing operation once the merger closed. I repeated what I had told him in our earlier Palo Alto meeting: it had to be my business model and my team. I had no intention of moving the company out of our headquarters, which were then located in Murray Hill, New Jersey, about 30 miles west of New York City.

In my capacity as CEO, I was spending an inordinate amount of time in Europe with our people and our global clients, and I wasn't about to extend travel time by five hours on each trip. Fine, he replied. We'll go with your business model, and you can stay put in New Jersey. But, he added, "I'd appreciate it if you would take some of HP Tech Finance on to your team." Which I did.

Frankly, I never thought I was auditioning for the job of CEO of this new financial services company. I genuinely felt my purpose that day with Wayman was to educate him as best I could on the financial services industry, how we had done our business at Compaq, and how any new HP venture could thrive. HP was top of the line when it came to building and marketing technology products. Not so much when it came to customer financing.

The truth of the matter is that HP Tech Finance ran on a very different model from what we had used. They didn't have an effective measurement system, and it seemed unclear what HP really wanted from this segment of its business. Did they want it to be a profit center, or did they want it to be something else? Were they a lender of last resort? A sales enabler? They finally decided on sales enabler. It's no wonder this approach produced mediocre results. Where would the motivation to perform emanate from?

Executives were rotated in and out; HP put employees in charge who they thought had potential, which makes some sense from a developmental standpoint. But as the head of a financial services company, it's far better to appoint a leader steeped in the financial services industry. HP Tech Finance was $7.5 billion in assets. Don't you want someone who knows the business to be in charge of an investment that size?

HP Tech Finance had made some decisions that didn't reflect my operational strategy. All the back-office operations for its Latin America businesses, for example, were in Canada. Made no sense to me at all. There was supposed to be some tax benefit associated with that decision, but we closed that office and some others scattered here and there. The back office should be centralized—that's the way I wanted it—and their operation was quite decentralized. Most of those employees were not offered opportunities to move once the merger was complete.

As a postscript to the conversation Bob Wayman and I had regarding HP's commitment to our model and location, we had another talk a few months later. The old HP Tech Finance setup had credit and collections performed by the corporate credit group under the auspices of the HP Controller, essentially the trade credit (30-60-90 days' exposure) guys who had little to no term credit (3-4-5 years' exposure) experience. Nor were they all that concerned about the financials of a round peg in a square-hole business unit that had "sales enabler" as a mission description . . . and the results showed it.

Our model was end to end, a fully integrated business that, of course, included credit and collections. What kind of finance company would we be otherwise? Though Wayman (and Fiorina) had agreed, the implementation sparked a palace revolt among Wayman's minions, especially the Controller's organization who (shockingly!) saw the decision as a give-up. "We don't know these Compaq guys. Who are they to come in and make demands? How do we know we can trust them?" They pretty much ignored their own track record as they protested.

Wayman never articulated as much, but I knew exactly what was going on, having participated in a few bouts of corporate infighting from time to time. Rather, Wayman, a smooth operator, called and said, "We're okay with your end-to-end business model, but we'd like to create an oversight committee, sort of like an internal board of directors. My finance team will sit on it."

I don't know what kind of reaction he was expecting, but I think he was surprised when I said, "Great!" (I've always been a believer in "Keep your friends close and your other friends (?) closer.") But why not make this internal board into a group that can really do HP Financial Services some good? In addition to the finance team, why don't we add the leaders of the HP business units to the board as well? That way we can be assured our go-to market will be in alignment with HP's strategic direction."

Bob said, "Good idea, let's go that route."

In the final minutes of that call, I sealed the deal that co-opted our finance team detractors.

Bob: Irv, you should be the board chairman.

Irv: No way, Bob. That should be your job.

Bob: Can't, too busy.

Irv: I can't believe you don't have a couple of hours per quarter for an $8 billion-plus investment.

Bob: You have a point. Okay.

I can't say everything was immediately sweetness and light, but the ambiance was dramatically altered. And we bought time to earn the trust of Wayman's team by performing at a high level as promised.

One of the reasons mergers and acquisitions fail is because, while close attention is paid to the numbers, they're too often overly optimistic about the numerical upside, on both sides of the consolidation—growth and expense savings. We talk about the future rate of growth, what we ought to be able to achieve if the stars fall into place. As for "synergies"—read *cost takeouts*—assumptions can be very aggressive, especially as in regard to timing. And then you draft a business plan that's too rosy and insufficiently rooted in business reality. You see that all the time.

The amount of time spent building a business case, whether it's the HP/Compaq merger or the integration of Compaq Financial Services and HP Tech Finance, often leaves out—or at least minimizes—consideration of the impact on the employees of both companies. There's a sum of X persons here and Y persons there, and those sums are going to be combined. Some reduction is inevitable. That certainly was the case with the home offices of HP and Compaq, where the postmerger body count ran high.

No question about it—the cultural implications of a merger of two major American companies, no matter how thorough the planning and how seamless the execution, cannot be underestimated. Once the papers are signed, you're left with people from two different organizations who are going to have to work together. As HP was retaining the name and the corporate branding, for many in the Compaq family it inevitably would be a difficult, even wrenching, transition.

It's not really something you can, or want to, delegate to Human Resources. HR is very good at some things: benefits plans, recruiting, efficient training programs. That's classic HR. Corporate assimilation is not. The ultimate differentiator is that HR, while an essential spoke in the company wheel, doesn't run a business.

And at the end of the day, when you're running a business, you've got to make your numbers as reflected in the business case. You can't walk away from the responsibility and hand off this enormous task to HR, wiping your hands clean in the process and ordering them to handle it.

In a nutshell, when two companies merge and you have to start blending two distinctive enterprises, you can't forget that there are different people, different objectives, different approaches to the marketplace, different approaches to the customers. But the guy sitting at the top of the business has to be worried about all of it—especially in a financial services business environment where it's the employees who do all the executing. No whiz-bang R&D is going to get the job done.

The period between announcement of a merger or acquisition and its finalization often involves teams from each side operating in a "clean room." This is designed to allow long-time rivals, soon to be brothers and sisters in one corporate family, to plan the integration without revealing key sensitive information to their future co-workers. This is, in essence, the first big step in the post merger planning. Lots of people from both HP and Compaq were placed on these clean-room teams.

In our case, this was especially critical. The HP/Compaq marriage was the computer industry's biggest merger to date. Smoothly combining distinct cultures, manufacturing, sales, and research operations was of paramount importance in making the transaction work. There are strict rules about what can and can't be exchanged, or divulged, in the clean-room period. The federal government is very prescriptive in this regard.

Within 30 minutes of the deal closing, however, I called Gary Silverman, our global head of credit, into my office and told him, "Get up to your elbows in that balance sheet, I want to know what the hell is going on." I didn't have a good feeling about the HP Tech Finance control environment. We put a team on it. A couple of weeks later, Gary stopped by and started to talk about the review. I could tell immediately from his body language that he wasn't the bearer of good news.

"Just give me the number," I said, referring to the amount of bad debt that remained on HP Tech Finance's books. "250," he said. Million, that is.

"Holy s—," I said. I got on the phone with Jon Flaxman, the controller of HP. "I had a team looking at the balance sheet, and you need to take another $250 million write-off," I said. This, of course, kicked up quite a bit of dust at the home office. After taxes, $250 million was $125 million in net income. It was bad credit from South America and elsewhere. Some of the deals had been on the books for two years or more, but they had never collected a dime nor written off a penny.

This was no way to run an airline. I told Jon, "You have to take this 250 hit." My name was mud for a while at HP headquarters, as though this was my fault. They had already written down $475 million before the deal closed, but that was at no cost (due to the wonders of purchase-money accounting). My attitude was, "Hey, don't shoot the messenger." We finally took the loss, and our results for the fiscal year ending October 31, 2002 were going to show a $125 million net income loss for the newly named and newly created Hewlett-Packard Financial Services. In September, I was summoned to talk to the finance committee of the HP board and discuss our forecast for 2003.

"Here's my business plan," I said. It projected a profit of $80 million, despite the enormous loss we were reporting for 2002. Patricia Dunn, a member of the HP board who would later serve as chairwoman, challenged our projections. She had come out of financial services and understood our business reasonably well. She was dubious, to say the least.

"Let me get this straight. You're going to lose $125 million this year, and next year you're going to make $80?" she asked, incredulously. "A $200-million net income turnaround in one year? How are you going to do that?"

"I understand how the portfolio works, I know what's in there now," I responded, "and I'm telling you this is the result I'm going to produce."

"I don't believe it," she said. I walked them through our plans and projections, trying to persuade her especially that our assumptions weren't unduly optimistic. After the meeting, her attitude was pretty much: "Your funeral."

I have to say, she was right about the number. We didn't make $80 million in FY 2003, as promised. We made $85 million.

★   ★   ★

Our experience with Hewlett-Packard Financial Services was different from what had happened almost five years earlier with the creation of Compaq Financial Services. We'd started that business with a clean sheet of paper. With the HP merger, I knew there were some things we'd have to redo. It turned out to be much more challenging than I had imagined.

Companies either come in and start stomping around in heavy boots, or they tread too lightly. The correct approach is somewhere in the middle, which is where I tried to be in 2002. Our attitude was "We respect everything you did before, but here is what HP wants from us now: they want a business that makes money." You have to make a rational case for the new business model. Then you've got to sell it.

With mergers, as someone who takes over an integrated business and has to really market what you're trying to do to a large number of anxious, doubtful employees, you've got to work your ass off. And so I did. Once the deal was finalized at the beginning of May 2002, making the case was pretty much all I did for the next 12 months—180 business days on the road.

I went to every corner of the earth. My message was as direct as I could make it. "This is what we're going to do, this is why we're doing it, and here's how we're going to accomplish it. Not the least of it," I told each of my audiences—Compaq holdovers and HP employees alike, across all of our regional offices—"is why you're going to like it." It wasn't a case of stomping around in big shoes, but somebody had to make it clear that what had gone before wasn't going to continue. We were going to run this like a real business, with a balance sheet and an understanding where the profit pools were. And we were, to a man and woman, going to like it.

Here's the thing to know in assessing the combination of these two major tech companies: it wasn't exactly a merger. HP was buying Compaq. In the parlance of the year 2002, you had the blue team and the red team. HP was the blue team, Compaq the red team. That is, except for Compaq Financial Services and HP Tech Finance. In the case of the two affected financial services enterprises, it really was a merger, two companies coming together as one.

We didn't do "here's HP's product line, with products A, B, C, D, and here's Compaq's product line, with products A, B, C and D." It wasn't a case of "shoot that product line, shoot this product line, close this factory, etc. . . . instead of having eight people to do it, let's have five." The new brand, the controlling business philosophy, and the operating structure were to be HP's. That isn't a merger. It's a takeover. Essentially, that's how the HP-Compaq deal transpired.

On our end, people started calling it a reverse merger, but the integration of HP Tech Finance and Compaq Financial Services still meant melding two diverse cultures and operating strategies. We couldn't completely avoid the musical chairs aspect of combining two big business operations. Of course, there was duplication, and we had to decide who would sit in what chair. Two people for the same job meant someone had to go.

But we didn't blow up product lines and fire 1,000 employees. We're a people business, and we kept that in mind as we proceeded. Unlike HP/Compaq hardware, for example, you can't simply walk down a production line and eliminate unnecessary functions.

As a leader, you want to be sensitive and understand the hardship employees endure when thrown into an unsettled situation. The financial services business, maybe more than any other business, is about those who work for you. We don't manufacture anything; we don't have the latest high-tech distribution model; we don't import or export anything. Whether we can execute better than the other guys makes the difference between success and failure—it's all about out executing the other guy.

Layoffs thinned some of the workforce, but most of the combined staff were absorbed. As requested following my meeting with Wayman, we had brought in people from HP, which meant

I had to tell some of my own people, "You didn't make the cut." That was painful.

*   *   *

Those were some of the thoughts that informed my thinking and my presentations on the road after the deal closed. I've always believed that the tone is set at the very top of the business. When people see that I'm on the road for 180 days, working diligently to get the message out, to answer the nervous questions and possibly ease the anxiety expressed in those faces staring back at me from the audience, I'm always hopeful we can have a meeting of the minds.

Sometimes you have to deliver messages you know are going to be hard to hear. But you always say what you have to say. During my world tour, I encountered hostility in some places. Paris, for instance. There was downright animosity when I addressed the troops of our French operation. Trying to effect change when people thought they had a job for life, as they usually do in France, Italy, Germany, and Spain and other places, can pose challenges in building a more responsive and reactive workplace mindset.

It took us some time to evolve in some of these countries, but now the naysayers are all gone. As I've said over the years to our European leadership, get the UK, France, and Germany knocked, and you are going to do well. Until that happens, the region won't perform to potential. These countries are 50 percent of the volume, and until you get things clicking on all cylinders there, you're not going to produce the results we want.

It all starts with the leadership. The leader we eventually installed in Germany struggled the first year but is now doing extremely well. Same for the woman who runs France for us. It took her a while to get going, but she too is doing a good job for us now. We hired organically. You can move people around, send senior managers from the United States to business locations abroad, but I'd much rather find a highly qualified national who can bring knowledge of the local business and social culture to running my region.

Put somebody in a leadership role who doesn't understand the country, and it can take three to six months, easy, to get up to speed. You relocate, and there's challenge in that alone. The family doesn't yet grasp the language, moms have to deal with everything new including schools for the kids. Nothing comes easily, and the business, even in the hands of the most competent leader, can suffer in the short term.

For us, post merger, the first year was very much about instilling in our team a new philosophy that channeled our global business needs. We wanted to create our own community, operating as one global company world-wide, working collaboratively in teams on a customer-in basis and driven by a single operational vision, regardless of the market or national location. Our objective was to base our decisions on our fiduciary responsibility to the shareholders of HP. We are not sales enablers. We were going to run this as a business.

Not everybody jumped immediately on board. After the merger, some people stayed and groused for a while and later departed. That's to be expected. A fair number of HP Tech Finance senior leaders made the transition, but most of them eventually left, too. The ones who stayed made important contributions. They were here because they wanted to be, and I always appreciate a sense of commitment exhibited under difficult, even jarring, circumstances.

I kind of feel the way the late New York Yankees owner George Steinbrenner did. If you don't want to be here, to be a part of something special, then we don't want you. But if you do, wear the uniform proudly.

*   *   *

A year into our new existence, I still felt as though we had things to prove. That's my DNA. When we posted that $85 million profit against all odds and expectations after our first year, did I start to feel comfortable in my corporate shoes? *Comfortable* is not a word in my lexicon. And I suspect it won't be, for as long as I continue in this role.

So much of it, for me, is making sure that I'm never too far from the action. As confident as you are in your senior leadership teams, there are times when you simply have to roll up your sleeves and take on a more direct client-service role, doing the work, getting your fingernails dirty.

Chapter 12

Getting Your Fingernails Dirty

Business leaders cannot ignore what's going on around them and survive. If you live in an ivory tower, you'll fail. It's that simple. Keeping yourself too detached from the essential give and take of your business is a recipe for disaster. Delegation of the day-to-day operations does make sense at a certain level. You put a talented, dedicated management team in place, and it would be a mistake for the organization—and a slap at the people you've entrusted to execute your mission at the highest levels—not to let them do their jobs and reach their individual potential.

Realistically, it's impossible to know every little detail of your enterprise, especially when you have 1,500 employees operating in more than 50 countries. But that doesn't mean you shouldn't immerse yourself in the most important aspects of business and performance.

Show me a leader who doesn't have dirty fingernails, and I'll show someone who probably won't be in the job very long. You have to thoroughly understand what's going on—the deals you're making or considering, deployment of your business model, customer satisfaction, and performance of the leadership team and sales staff. My approach to oversight may be aggressive at times, but it's vital. It's also part of my nature; I don't think I could change it even if I wanted to, which I don't. Dan McCarthy likes to say, "Irv is built for speed, not for comfort." I think that's an apt description.

There's just no substitute for diving into the key details yourself. Sounds overly simple, but I'm constantly amazed at how little some executives seem to know about what's really going on in the trenches. Not me. I want and need to know the important details, especially when it comes to hearing and absorbing bad news, what we're going to do about our problem children, and assessing any negative fluctuations in the business.

To avoid falling out of touch with these pivotal areas, you need to establish some type of review cadence. Accountability is crucial. Check-in meetings must be on the calendar regularly. Be consistent when it comes to these meetings and what you hope to accomplish. At Hewlett-Packard Financial Services, we always use a template so that all the participants know exactly what will be covered and can prepare accordingly.

I have regularly calendared meetings with my direct reports—my senior leadership team—individually several times a month. We always know the topic of discussion in advance, and I expect us to stick to the program. That said, we leave time for ad hoc subjects, and my team knows I'm otherwise available to them 24/7. That's a guiding principle any chief executive must embrace;

be available, even if it interferes with other considerations, work or play.

Our CFO and I review the performance of the business units monthly, but there's always a forecast due or an interim result to consider. We often go deep into identifying and charting those elements that drive our key results. Those are the scheduled meetings, anyway. He and I are likely to talk far more frequently about the financial state of the business in a more informal setting. A day when we're not in each other's offices four or five times is rare. I wouldn't have it any other way.

It's an interesting line you must walk as a manager. Too much hands on and you're micromanaging; too little, and you could find yourself leafing through the want ads. I purposely don't chair any of our internal governance committees—credit, pricing, expansion, and so forth. But I am an active member of all of them and am careful to be the last to discuss the issues and cast my vote.

Of course, I have absolute veto power, as any engaged CEO should, but I try to use it sparingly if at all. We've created a system of clear-cut rules about quorums. I trust my team. If I can't make a meeting, decisions still get made. But it's up to me to make sure I get the homework afterward. We're in a fluid, fast-paced business. For all the attention to personnel and operational processes, I'm an absolute bugger when it comes to the business plan. To me, it's probably most the important management tool.

When I was CFO of AT&T Capital, my oft-used expression was "the business plan is inviolate." I still believe that, maybe even more now. We really put the organization through its paces when it comes to creating the plan. Our job as leaders is to grow the company; does the business plan have the requisite amount of stretch? If leaders have a plan that is too ambitious and likely to set up their team, as well as themselves, for failure, you need to recognize that, too, and be able to dial them back.

Typically, the staff is more interested in submitting what I like to call a rocking chair plan. That is, they can deliver it while relaxing. That won't do, and it's when I really kick into high gear. Testing their assumptions, challenging their conservative approaches, casting light on the deficiencies in their rationales—that's the responsibility of a leader who understands that growing the business means *growing* the business, not settling for complacency and less-than-optimal results.

To me, plans that are too long-range are cause for skepticism. But I do believe in setting long-term business objectives and developing a framework for the trajectory we need to get there. Remember this—a plan that extends out a year or two is more reliable. What's critically important is that the strategy and resultant plan match up seamlessly. Growth rates, operating ratios, and the "drop"—are you growing revenue by 10 percent but the bottom line only by 5 percent? Something's wrong! All of those elements must align to produce a high-quality, executable plan.

Our team tracks achievement against plan. We scrupulously manage by and measure against the plan we've built—think back to those review sessions I mentioned earlier. If you're an executive working for me and you're falling behind plan, you'd better come prepared with defensible remedies. On the flip side, if you're ahead of the plan, assess what's working well, what got you to that point, and make sure we can sustain or even build upon it.

It isn't as though these are formal gatherings. They're working sessions, with critiques, a healthy back and forth. We have a format, and we walk through it. I can't know every little thing that goes on in the business, but I know what I have to know. And I'm always ready to roll up my sleeves. I'm willing to get my fingernails dirty.

The bottom line is this: know what's going on. What are the expectations you've set for your people? Are they meeting those expectations? You have to operate with a model everyone can understand and apply. I want people who want the same things I want. You've got to want to grow the business. It's about ambitious targets, it's about stretch. You cannot work for me if good enough is good enough. We want to be world class; we want to be top dog. We don't have to step all over people to get there. But if you're not willing to extend yourself and take some risk, to stick your neck out, you may fall short.

★　　★　　★

There can be a lot of demands on my time, and I can't be in all places at once. But there are still times when my presence, or that of any leader, is critical. Sometimes it helps to be sitting at the table, ensuring that the deal gets done under the best possible circumstances for the company, as well as for the long-term benefit of our client. Call that rolling up your sleeves, or getting dirt under your nails. There are moments when the presence of the boss definitely pays real dividends.

To me, getting the chance to deal directly with our most important clients is still the best part of the job. I never like to be trotted out at social functions, for example, just to work the room. That's not me. But pitching a new line of business to a current or prospective client is the most rewarding thing I get to do.

As the great spy novelist, John Le Carré, once wrote, "A desk is a dangerous place from which to view the world." I couldn't agree more. Two examples of how I needed to interact directly with customers, and the difference I believe those face-to-face contacts made in sealing deals, come to mind.

During a trip to South Korea, I was to visit with one of our clients. Korea is somewhat like Japan in that they have these very large and powerful trading houses, *keiretsus* in Japan, *chaebols* in Korea. This particular client prefers to negotiate us down to the sixth decimal point. We make very little margin, but it's an important customer for Hewlett-Packard.

So I'm in Korea, we're going to see the customer. And I'm saying to the members of the Asia-Pacific team—our regional managing director, sales director, and Korean account representative—"Why me? Why do I have to see this customer?" I really believed the whole thing was kind of a waste of time, given the miniscule revenues from that account.

We arrived at the trading house in Seoul. Lots of smiling faces, the usual niceties. Steam was coming out of my ears. I was smiling but thinking, "What the hell am I doing here?" I had to think of some way of profiting from this meeting, so during our conversation, I asked the company's senior vice-president of finance, "By the way, what do you do with all the equipment you finance with us when the lease is fully amortized?"

Puffing up his chest, he proudly said, "We donate most of it to schools, orphanages, hospitals . . ."

"That's interesting," I said. "What are you doing to scrub the hard drive before you donate it?"

A pause. The Korean executive stared at me. "We don't actually do anything about it."

"So, your customer information, business strategy, payroll information, all your key information—some second grader has it on his desk?"

"I guess so," he said sheepishly.

Finally, a glimmer of light. "If HPFS was handling your asset disposition at the expiration of the lease, we could make sure this doesn't happen," I said. "I'm sure we can work a deal, work something out."

So we managed to reach a new business arrangement, something that would take us from negotiating to the sixth decimal place to actually making some real money. I wondered why we hadn't pursued this promising path until now. I couldn't resist needling our regional sales director in the elevator after leaving the meeting.

"How come I have to have this conversation with the guy?" I asked. In reality, it's these kinds of moments that remind me how satisfying it is to seal a deal.

That held true during a trip to São Paolo that began under similar circumstances. São Paolo is overcrowded, congested, chaotic. More than 20 million Brazilians live in the city proper or just outside its borders. There are less than 40 miles of train rail. City traffic is so bad it can take hours to travel from one side of the city to the other. It's not unusual for somebody to be an hour late or an hour early to a meeting. It's understood and accepted.

We began this particular day with a meeting at General Motors Brazil. When we finished and left the building, the sun was shining, a lovely day. Told we would have to head to the heliport for the ride across town to the next meeting, I was puzzled. Why not drive, I asked our Brazilian sales leader?

"We could, but it would take two and a half, three hours to get there," he said. "The helicopter will take us 20 minutes."

The last thing I wanted to do was take a chopper, especially with only one guy in the driver's seat. Then again, I didn't have three hours to kill or the patience to sit in traffic. So up we went. There are more helicopters in Sao Paulo per square mile, I'm certain, than in any other city in the world. The place is abuzz with them. Three hundred office buildings have helipads on the roof. Within minutes, the beautiful weather was gone, replaced by sudden, violent thunderstorms. It indeed took 20 minutes to get across town, but it wasn't a pleasant ride.

The pilot set us down on the roof of the 50-story building where our next meeting was scheduled, with Brazil's second-largest mobile phone company. We slid out of the bird, battling what seemed like gale force winds. The footing was slick, like the

Madison Square Garden rink during hockey season. I clambered out and was nearly blown off the roof.

Minutes later, we were seated at the table—our Latin America head of sales, the account representative, and me. Their treasurer was with us. We wanted to do business with this company, and it was important enough to bring the boss along for what should be a good negotiation, real give and take between me and my team and their CFO. Why else would I be there?

The CFO kept us waiting. Finally, he strode into the room and sat down. He slipped his watch from his wrist and placed it on the table. "Thank you very much for coming. When we do have something, we are going to a discounted cash flow analysis, and if the numbers come out right, we'll do a deal with you."

And with that, he replaced his watch, rose, and began to leave the conference room. Having survived the chopper of death and done my best Wayne Gretzky imitation on the rooftop, I was not having any of it.

"I can certainly appreciate that's a way to think about it," I told him.

"But you know, you're never going to do business with us. My money isn't cheap enough for you. But if you'll be good enough to give me another couple of minutes, I'm going to explain to you how I can add value to your business."

That piqued his interest. I directed him from Point A to Point B of the HPFS value proposition. A half hour later, he was still listening. We walked out of that meeting with a deal to lease them servers and other infrastructure. In all, we'd be looking at four separate deals and, most important, a customer relationship based on what value we could bring to the table—my kind of sales call. The lesson is that getting your fingernails dirty with a customer is about actually *getting your fingernails dirty with a customer.*

Chapter 13

Transforming Your Business

Y ou can never rest on your laurels. If there's one thing I've learned as a leader over the years, it's *adapt or die*. The graveyards of businesses long gone overflow with executives who got fat, became complacent, and lost their competitive edge. Self-satisfaction is a potential death sentence.

Changing course is never easy. Adapting to the shifting needs of an insistent marketplace sometimes requires tough choices across the board. I've had to upset the apple cart from time to time in order to ensure that our people and our business stay ahead of the pack. It hasn't always been universally supported. But you can never think of your stewardship of a multibillion-dollar company as a popularity contest. "Nice guys finish last."

If I sit back contentedly and think we're not only meeting but surpassing expectations—even when all signs point in that direction—two things can happen. I can watch as our more aggressive competitors zoom by us on the outside, leaving us behind and vulnerable. Or I can see to it that we fix things that still need fixing, even if it causes short-term unhappiness for my leadership team or our people as a whole. Andy Grove, one of the founders of Intel, has observed that "only the paranoid survive." It's a comment to which I fully and enthusiastically subscribe.

We've been fortunate in one sense. We've had the Hewlett-Packard balance sheet to back us up over the years, so we never had to worry about funding. That said, we had to manage the business well, and the economic calamity of the past several years made that as difficult a job as I've ever encountered.

However, even before the Great Recession threw a nasty wrench into the global business engine, I was concerned. We spent the first several years after the HP/Compaq merger getting the business to a place where we could be successful. But our performance between 2003 and 2006 was only okay. We needed to align our strategic direction with that of the parent company, and HP was struggling. I wasn't satisfied being the caretaker of a business, which is what I was starting to think I was. We needed to sit down and take a long hard look at ourselves in the mirror. We wanted to do better; Mark Hurd, who had been named CEO of HP in 2005 after the sacking of Carly Fiorina, wanted us to do better.

Unlike his predecessor, who had a background in marketing and was great at floating grand plans but less competent at running the business and keeping stakeholders happy, Hurd was focused on the bottom line and efficiency. I brought my team together. It was tough medicine time.

"Let's establish a stretch goal. Let's commit to a trajectory over the next couple of years to get us there." I said. "Let's have stuff that is truly actionable, implementable and let's agree to collective accountability for success."

Part of the plan was growing the business at double-digit rates. I didn't come in armed with paperwork forecasting a potential 20 percent bump. We needed growth in the neighborhood of 10 to 12 percent. I realized we couldn't grow our business at 20 percent. I knew that would never happen, my team knew that would never happen—not without taking ridiculous credit losses. And it wasn't strictly about growth anyway; it was about balancing growth and profitability.

You can always stand in front of the organization and say, "Hey, guess what! We're going to grow the business at 20 percent next year!"

And they're going to look at you and say, "What?!? Have you lost your mind?"

You need to create a plan that is a stretch but reasonable, that makes people uncomfortable but doesn't discourage them to the point of having them raise the white flag right from the beginning. The last thing you want your people to take away is the idea that we can never get there, so why even try? Keeping people on their toes by giving them challenging, but realistic goals is a key component of any successful enterprise.

Our business transformation strategy, we decided, would probably need a few years of steady improvement to get us operating on a world-class level. We worked with Hurd and his team on executing on the overall HP vision, getting a better understanding of how they were competing and would continue to compete in the marketplace. That way, we'd have something concrete to measure our performance against.

We emerged from these early discussions with four pillars of transformative change. Hewlett-Packard Financial Services had to grow its financing volume at a double-digit, but not 20 percent, rate. That was clear to me. We had to make some choices, some of them bound to be unpopular and anxiety inducing, about how we would deploy and manage the sales force. We had to improve sales force productivity as well: higher quotas and more sales people achieving at or better than quota. We had to emphasize the asset-management side of the business, because it had become increasingly obvious that asset management had substantial long-term profit potential.

And we had to achieve a significantly higher level of operating efficiency for the back office; we were going to put back-office operations under the microscope. Back office was a huge undertaking, it represented almost 50% of our total expense budget—and I was convinced we could do a far better job from a productivity standpoint.

We had much to do. New performance mandates were introduced. My thought was "Let's weed out the mediocre and replace them with more aggressive, competent employees. Let's talk about hitting productivity markers. Let's talk about how exactly we're going to make asset management a mainstream part of the business, instead of an afterthought."

As a rule of thumb, a chief executive can never forget this: everything you do as the leader of your business has a systemic implication. One high-level decision directly impacts another piece of the business, and so on across the board. Asset management becoming a priority raises the questions of how you're going to pay for it and whether it will mean diminished resources for other, more established but perhaps lesser-performing sides of the business.

When it comes to asset management, we probably made a questionable organizational decision at the start. It was set up originally as a separate business. We didn't have the right forward-thinking perspective to understand the importance of integrating asset management with sales. As our notion of value proposition really started to take form, and the thinking around it evolved in terms of how it could differentiate us in the marketplace, our strategy and tactical approaches necessarily evolved as well.

Under our transformation model, we were redirecting the sales force, which meant compensating them differently because we'd be focusing them on account relationships rather than the more conventional geographic territories. They needed to have the proper tools and training to succeed. You have to ensure that the asset-management team is delivering what the sales team is selling. Transforming a business is a blueprint for deep, multilayered, even initially unwieldy change. If you get wrong a single one of the five or six things you have to do, it could all come tumbling down like a house of cards.

An essential part of this process is finding the right people to direct the implementation of institutional change, who can both lead and collaborate.

★　　★　　★

Hewlett-Packard manages its international businesses through regional operations across the globe. We do the same. Our markets mirror theirs. For a company our size, you want to attract country leadership that understands the customer base and potential for growth, has a grasp of the quality and experience of the available labor pool, and knows both the national and business cultures.

Nevertheless, when we announced that the business model that had been in use for years was about to be updated for 2008 and beyond, it caused a stir, not only in our New Jersey headquarters, but around the world. This new plan was gut wrenching for certain employees in our operation, here and abroad. Our regional teams were end to end, they reported to regional leadership. Only our asset management business reported directly to one of my key senior executives in the United States, Gerri Gold.

A meeting of the HPFS leadership team was scheduled for a conference room outfitted with an easel holding an oversized pad of white paper. As the meeting came to order, I started writing: "This is exactly what the new business model will look like; this is how our management structure regionally and otherwise will be aligned." It was a no-nonsense meeting. I wasn't giving them a whole lot of room to negotiate and maneuver. It was my way or the highway.

"The back office, which we refer to as customer delivery isn't going to be reporting to you anymore," I said.

To say that was hard for many of them to swallow is short of understatement. In managing the back office, they were sitting on a big pot of operating capital. The money that we saved by moving some operations from Dublin into Wroclaw and in moving out of Sydney completely for Kuala Lumpur cut costs, so expanding into markets that offered us the promise of spending reductions was a key element. But the whole structure was inefficient, and since it was one of the four pillars of our transformative strategy, we were sure we had to get better control of it.

Our regional leaders were sitting on top of their individual empires, and now we were telling them they would become a glorified sales business. Go to market was the priority. Sales and asset management had to work together smoothly and more efficiently. Back-office productivity had to increase significantly over three years. We needed to find these productivity improvements across our three regions, which were managing according to different and sometimes incompatible standards.

My message was clear—we were going to be consistent around the world. And this is how we were going to do it.

Not everyone was willing to go along. Our executive in charge of the Americas region came into my office some time after the transformation was announced and told me he was leaving. Say whatever you want, I don't want anybody here that doesn't want to be here. Some of our regional leaders thought of themselves as emperors of all they surveyed. That approach was being cast into the scrap heap, and of course, there would be some repercussions.

Our business transformation coincided with the economic downturn that would engulf the U.S. and global markets starting in 2008. Did I foresee the financial tsunami about to wash over us all? Not really. At least not the extent to which it would drown us only a few months down the line. But if you looked around at how people were making money, you knew it had the potential to cause us real financial harm.

In times like these, it's just a question of whether you want to be fat, dumb, and happy and make as much money as you can. In fact, I'd argue that was a business strategy employed by far too many executives. Turning a blind eye to the rotting foundation while admiring the financial gold piled on top isn't my idea of responsible leadership.

Certainly, that wasn't my strategy. We were seeking operating efficiencies well in advance of the Great Recession. As we layered in our modified operating model, the objective was to increase productivity, streamline the business, and, at the same time, keep layoffs to a minimum, if we had to lay anyone off at all. We had to improve the back office. We had to be more efficient. We had to grow sales at a double-digit rate. We required bigger contributions from our asset management business, already a high-margin business.

In order to do that, we had to save money here and here, so that we could invest more money in our go-to-market push. This was not only a formula for enhancing the business; it turned out to be a strong prescription for riding out the recession in the latter part of the decade.

By raising sales quotas, one of the staples of our new plan, we were cherry picking the top producers and offering them incentives for meeting our new standards. We started pruning the producers at the bottom. If you couldn't cut it, you probably needed to go. That was true of sales leadership as well. I'm sure that injected higher levels of stress into our sales team, but that was the way it had to be. Many left and weren't replaced. We dealt with the economy largely by losing people through attrition, to me a far preferable solution to enacting outright job cuts.

I required everyone with an assignment to report back to me every week. I was convinced it was the right thing to do for the company. Despite the trepidation, it succeeded. Customer satisfaction went up. Expenses went down. Productivity went up. Accounts receivable went down. Losses as a percentage of assets stayed flat, at market leading and acceptable levels.

You can't ask for anything more than that when you impose a sweeping new system, particularly one that challenges assumptions about the best means of running the company. This was designed as a three-year overhaul, running through the end of our 2010 fiscal year, and I have to commend the team we've assembled at Hewlett-Packard Financial Services. They did a hell of a job, taking the ball and running with it.

Not everybody responds as you hope they will. Some will decide to vote with their feet, which is okay. I'm not big on demoting people. Sometimes I might believe it's smart to get rid of certain people, but they retain a body of knowledge that's still of great value to the company, maybe just not in their current position. In rare cases, we might move some people around to take advantage of the positives they do bring.

The recent recession was instructive in terms of sharpening employees' focus on their performance, forcing them to perform better. As with all down economic cycles, there are glimmers of opportunity. The best and brightest, not only at HPFS but at any enterprise, take advantage of them. We all went through change together. But you can't look at the guy across the street and use that as strict comparison. It's about how it affects you personally.

My old basketball coach used to say, "Don't get too high in victory, don't get too low in defeat." That's an important part of my business philosophy. When things are going great guns, money's pouring in and new customers are coming online, that's the ideal. But don't let it go to your head. And when we are being lashed by the harsh winds of recession, hunker down, take care of business the best you can, and understand that calmer days will return.

You are going to celebrate your wins, and you are going to suffer your losses. However, it pays to keep things within a manageable range. Keep things in perspective.

I don't think you can look too far down the road. Too many things are subject to market corrections and directions beyond our control. We make a five-year plan, mostly to set a trajectory in place, but we rarely go beyond two years in actual planning and implementation. Our most recent transformation plan took us through 2008–2010.

Is there a new round of transitional changes on the horizon? I would almost guarantee there is. We have new leadership at HP, a new CEO whose background is in consumer products and services rather than the hardware business that has defined the company since its inception.

The philosophy on building, maintaining, and even reducing staff is uncomplicated. You get rid of low achievers, but avoid layoffs unless it is practically impossible to avoid them. Build quality without losing numbers. The market is constantly changing and adapting. It's dynamic and demanding. You can't blind yourself to it. But still, we've always tried to maintain our staffing numbers as long as our workers remained competent and contributed—and as long as they felt a sense of shared ownership and common objectives.

I think one of the keys to carrying out any significant transformation is not only having to weigh the pros and cons of altering departments, divisions, work plans, and operating strategies. A key is spending wisely during the process. You commit funds to smart things. You invest in technology, in things that absolutely help your business. Training is an essential investment. Trouble is, that's occasionally been a bone of contention with the home office.

At one point, after we had submitted a budgetary request for additional training money, the head of human resources challenged me on it. "You're spending too much on training," she insisted. My response was fairly simple: "How do you know?" Some elements of budget setting are clear. And there are some, like investing in talent, nurturing their skills, and creating a better, more productive work force, that you can't adequately measure only by how much you spend on it.

With any overarching operational change, you have to think ahead, obviously. People have to step up to things that they don't necessarily know or haven't done before. The ones who are capable of doing that will shine. Cream rises to the top. Demanding levels of performance from ourselves that may reach far north of where we've been, or thought we could be, is natural for any leader if he or she brings full confidence and conviction to the task.

Chapter 14

Communicating
the Message

How do you make a big company small? How do you
bridge gaps that inevitably develop from doing business
in disparate cultural, political, and financial environ-
ments? Tough questions, indeed. Any chief executive who runs a
business aspiring to lasting financial success on a global scale better
be able to answer them, though, or at least fashion a framework
that promotes the best possible solutions. These are formidable
challenges.

As we built Compaq Financial Services and later Hewlett-
Packard Financial Services into truly global enterprises, there
was no shortage of obstacles to overcome. Yet one of the most

important lessons from the past three decades is that making the big and potentially unwieldy seem smaller and more interconnected, depends intrinsically on how you communicate with your people, customers, investors, and corporate boards. That requires an ability to deliver your corporate message both internally *and* externally.

Now more than ever, communications is a fundamental responsibility of the company leader. Marshall McLuhan, the noted educator, writer, and cultural critic from the 1960s and 1970s, coined a phrase that for many defined the fast-changing world of communication nearly a half-century ago: "The medium is the message." And that's when the media pretty much consisted only of newspapers, magazines, radio, and a limited number of network and local television broadcasters.

Clearly, we've moved well beyond McLuhan's age-old aphorism. The simple days of print and broadcast media seem light years ago. In fact, I'd suggest the flip side of the McLuhan message holds more true today—"The message is the medium." With the meteoric rise over the past decade of product- and service-specific branding as an organizing business principle, creating a durable, attractive message that can then be distributed widely through the ever-expanding arteries of old media, digital media, and social media is a core value.

There are messaging groups that stand above all—the Hewlett-Packard organization, in the form of business groups, divisions, and sales units; direct contact with customers either live when I travel or through electronic means; and finally, providing effective messaging for the employees of Hewlett-Packard Financial Services.

Communicating with the HPFS team begins with a broad internal communications strategy. Different companies communicate in very different ways with their people. Some executives continue to share their thinking primarily through voicemail messages, or by e-mailing in the style of "notes from the corner office" or similar communiqués.

We certainly subscribe to traditional forms of message dissemination, but we—as so many other companies in financial services and elsewhere—are really just beginning to stick our collective toe into the social media pond. Moving away from communicating with big groups toward linking broader audiences in real time is something we're embracing.

Social networking has become a common means of communication for virtually every enterprise. I'm very old school in a lot of ways, but I've never been shy about doing anything and everything it takes to keep our company pushing ahead. New age, to me, means any modern, effective method of transmitting our mission and what our people stand for to the widest possible audience. Our communications team is continually preaching to me the value of using new and evolving digital media to advance our collective cause, and I'm open to these ideas.

When it comes to social media, somebody else can decide what's old school or new school. It may not be the most comfortable thing in the world—especially for those of us who've been in the business a long time and grew up professionally having to worry mostly about word of mouth internally and print media externally as the principle conduits of corporate news, but if it's important to the company, you do it.

Still, I like best of all the fact that we talk at least once every three months to our people across the scores of HPFS offices in the United States and abroad and much more frequently than that in small groups as opportunities arise. Our quarterly town hall meetings afford me the opportunity to spend quality time with the people who keep our engines humming. The concept may be quaint to some who are dismissive of old-fashioned ways of team interactions, but I find it stimulating and something I look forward to.

Certain guiding rules apply when conducting formal large-scale meetings with your employees. First, never sugarcoat the news. I stand up there, and I tell them what's what. I give them the good, the bad, and the ugly. I've found throughout my career, from my earliest days in sales to my stewardship of a multibillion-dollar company, that the "everything is great" speech should be avoided.

Commending and saluting your people is important. Our recent annual numbers *have* been very good, and I'm always quick to recognize the fine work of all our teams. But even in past years when our overall results weren't all that great, it was important to remember that somebody, somewhere, was doing a bang-up job that deserved to be highlighted and praised. It provides some measure of uplift even when the news tends to be more sobering across the entire enterprise.

And there will always come a time when the news will be sobering, whether it's declining revenues or a wider crisis within the industry. Making sure the best of the best receive that recognition for a job well done, regardless of the company's macro performance, is an essential part of communicating the message.

Ours is an intensely competitive industry. We collide daily with behemoths like GE Capital. Being forthright and candid with employees about the market obstacles ahead of us, and what it means to them personally and as a unit, is paramount. I need to remind them in the most direct terms of the challenges that continue to present themselves. That goes for all of us, whether it's a senior vice-president or brand new salesperson.

As part of a recent global kickoff meeting, we featured a series of interactive exercises designed to connect us better to our workers. One of the exercises was conducting a chat room conversation with the boss—that would be me. I hosted this online talk for an hour or so, and we had great fun with it. I found the whole process invigorating. People waited in line for quite a while to participate, which I found especially gratifying and expressive of wide interest in what we were doing and trying to accomplish.

Now, I'm not much of a typist. So I hunted and pecked my way through this particular meeting. But our communications director, Jennifer Marinaro, reported that the response was, in her words, phenomenal, far better than anyone expected. I'm thinking we'll be looking at the "Chat with Irv" segments as a spoke in our ongoing communications wheel in the years ahead, and I'm happy to be a part of it.

These interactive channels, I have to confess, are not only enjoyable, but also extremely useful for a chief executive. You find things you can take away from each session, times when you think, "Y'know, I hadn't thought of that," or employees' ideas that are genuinely helpful. It varies according to where you are. When I'm in Malaysia, the audience tends to be a little more reserved. In Sydney, well, reserved isn't the word I'd use for our Aussie brothers and sisters. The Australian team, on the whole, is more outspoken. Different cultures respond in ways that are comfortable for them; it's up to me to recognize that and handle it accordingly. It's another reason we encourage small, local meetings.

This goes back to basic communications, really. It's not so far different from the conversations that might occur around the dinner table. The main consideration is making sure the messages gain the same foothold in Dublin as they do in Poland or Kuala Lumpur. The company message has to be delivered in terms that are acceptable by, and understandable to, employees speaking different languages and living in places where they are subject to different work rules, compensation levels, and corporate structure. This is a challenge that never abates, but it's part and parcel of maintaining a competitive global enterprise, with all the difficulties that entails.

We often have to deal with cultural issues beyond language. I think things are improving in that regard; it's about executing and determining exactly how our message is delivered from our global headquarters.

I'm also smart enough to not to say anything that will be misconstrued or just sound stupid when I'm addressing the troops. Sometimes there are questions such as "It's taken me three months to get a replacement printer, can you help me?" Of course, when you get something like that, you just tell them that's a level of detail you don't have. "But come see me after the meeting, and we'll try to figure out a solution."

More often, I get questions about emerging markets. Where are we going next? and what should they expect in their particular markets or countries? To name just two. I routinely tell them we'll make an informed decision taking all socioeconomic conditions into account. Our mission at home and abroad is to support Hewlett-Packard principally, but we're always going to be examining the big picture.

★   ★   ★

High-quality executive communications isn't just the responsibility of the chief executive, corporate president, or board chairman. Your senior leadership team, to a man and woman, must be fully subscribed to the corporate mission and able to articulate it effectively. I'm not talking about some sort of preaching or proselytizing, but having everybody on the same page is integral to effective communication.

There also has to be consistency in your delivery. Some years back, we implemented a business transformation plan. I thought we needed to do a better job, be more adaptive to changing market and customer demands. We sent everybody to the drawing board with orders to come back with their best thinking to help facilitate the transformation. I wanted to make sure my message was clear.

"I don't want your Christmas list, but we have a few holes in the dyke," I told one of my most senior people. "I want you to be able to execute against the plan." Some of it was essentially moving existing resources from one area to the next for more efficient deployment. We were, in a way, robbing Peter to pay Paul.

One of our senior guys came in with a long, elaborate presentation. "You're boiling the ocean," I replied. That phrase, for those unfamiliar with some of the language of the corporate decision-making world, pretty well sums up the taking of something that should be relatively simple and inflating it into a project of enormous and perhaps needless complexity. And in this case, the ocean was steaming.

My own message was simple: Give me three or four things you're going to do in 2011, three or four things you want to do in 2012, and where we are going to be in terms of capacity and quality. How will these proposals fit into our overall strategy to address and satisfy the most insistent needs of our customers? The lesson is that, when it comes to steering a company through significant structural change, keep it as simple as possible. You can give me an extensive list of goals and objectives, and you may have captured the essence of how we as an executive team will expect to grow the business. Enumerate too many objectives, and you run the risk of not being able to do any of them.

Few would disagree that Ronald Reagan was one of the most successful presidents of the twentieth century. It was often said of Reagan that he achieved that stature by concentrating on no more than a few key policy initiatives. And, of course, he was *nonpareil* when it came to communicating his policy imperatives, using language both precise and direct. He was an uncomplicated speaker, but his message was always forceful and clear. He had a knack for inspiring the best in people. His acknowledgment of the national need for "Morning in America" near the start of his presidency after the struggle of the Carter years was instructive.

As business executives, there is no reason we should aspire to anything less. You have to be able to talk to your own direct reports in terms that are equally precise, pointed, and easy to embrace. We've got three, four, maybe five things to get done. This is how we'll do them. No muss, no fuss. Through your executive team, you must delineate roles and assignments clearly and intelligently, so they can be handed down in productive ways. You can grind the business to a halt if you don't differentiate tasks. Some plans are too amorphous, asking too many employees to do the same things. Everyone needs to understand his or her role and what is expected of it.

I want solutions that leave a meaningful, positive mark. For me, it's always been a question of simplification and clarity. Break it down to specifications that are actionable and hold the highest promise of successful implementation. Any message I transmit to HPFS employees should be about impact on them—"This is what we are going to do, this is why we are going to do it, and this is what it will mean to you."

Show me a PowerPoint slide presentation that's 50 or 75 pages long, and I'll show you a sure-fire way to put people to sleep. That's another case of boiling the ocean. You risk losing the very people you're trying to coerce or convince; they can become discouraged and lose heart—and that's before you even get to Slide 3.

If you come right out and explain that these are the four things we're going to do and how we will do them, that this is your role and how it's going to positively affect your careers at Hewlett-Packard Financial Services, then you've got people sitting on the edges of their seats and listening attentively. Simplify, capture the message, express it clearly—you're more likely to find your audience nodding in agreement. Leonardo da Vinci said that "simplicity is the ultimate sophistication." Who could argue?

Understand this as well: not every plan you write down on the whiteboard is going to work. That's a fact of business life, and no one—not Jack Welch, not Warren Buffett, not Bill Gates—is immune to the occasional misstep. A lot of people don't understand that basic precept. They may believe that any sign of failure means the sun won't be coming out tomorrow. We're not a monopoly in the leasing and financing world; few if any companies claim complete domination of their markets. You just aren't going to win them all.

But the basic lessons of communicating with those who work for you—delivering an easy-to-digest message, repeating it as frequently as possible, sticking to the facts and the truth, and not sugarcoating anything—provide an informational transparency that both illuminates the issues and consolidates support for strategic and tactical missions. Things need to be in balance. Your employees need to understand what you're doing and why. You always want them to rally around the company, and you want to be able to explain to them why they should be willing to do so.

For the past several years, we've been setting stretch targets. We've achieved and shot right past those targets. Part of it is building excitement. My professional motivations might be far different from those of my peers and competitors. If somebody tells me, for example, you've got to get from X to Z—from $50 million income, say, to $100 million—I could get excited about that. Now, I'm not sure everyone at HPFS will feel exactly the same way. But we're continually thinking: How can we get people excited about something else that would be meaningful to them?

★   ★   ★

Communicating effectively involves a different set of parameters internally than dealing with the outside business world through external media outlets. The assumption is when speaking with employees that there's a shared sense of purpose. You've built up a level of trust. Our folks are invested in our success and hang on every development. Together, we are all pushing against the wheel to steer our enterprise in the right direction for the benefit of managers, staff, and more broadly, Hewlett-Packard and its shareholders.

When it comes to the media, all bets are off. From my years as a chief executive working for high-profile companies that have had their moments out of the media sun, I think I can offer one piece of basic advice: Keep your nose clean and your head down. Lots of corporate executives love the limelight; they can't wait to see their words quoted in the *Wall Street Journal* or their pearls of market wisdom broadcast on CNBC. Not me. More often than not, it's something to avoid. I don't want to be on the front page of the *Journal*—unless I win the $350 million lottery. If I do that, feel free to splash my story all over the cover.

Yet there's a dichotomy. We're in a world where communication is instant. We're all stuck in a 24/7 multimedia grinder. When I started running businesses on a global scale—and I'm going back to the late 1980s—there was no Internet. Cable news was still in its infancy. For a captive finance company, there may not be a lot of Page One press, but we still have to be considerate of media demands and acknowledge the pressures. Externally, our world is Hewlett-Packard. So we do need to focus on getting our word out when it behooves the parent company or facilitates the needs of HPFS.

We're not the kind of company that's going to take out an ad in *BusinessWeek*. We care about HP and HP customers, so the external communication focus is rooted in messaging that enlightens and serves our customers, clarifies our mission statement to the outside world, and promotes both current and future expectations of business success. If our innovation and quality of leadership catch on with the business press, better still.

During my years at the helm of major global businesses—AT&T Capital, later Compaq Financial Services and HPFS—we've been fortunate in that regard. From our positive portrayal all those years ago in the *New York Times,* when they saluted the operating model we'd adopted as it matured through the 1980s, to more recent, complimentary reviews in large regional newspapers and important trade publications, we have effectively managed our dealings with the press and, for the most part, have benefited from them.

Having good press is important to any large-scale organization. It's a signal to the industry and the markets that exceptional work is being done. It builds the interest of prospective customers and often cements existing business relationships. No question, it lifts employee morale, and that's a piece that is never insignificant. A favorable profile or analysis in leading media is a source of great pride throughout the company.

During my days in the Army Reserves, I had an old drill sergeant who loved to say, "You have to have your shit grouped." When you train with the M-16 firearm in basic training, you're asked to hit a very small circle in the middle of the target some distance away. You use an eight-round clip. The result of discharging that clip at the target is the shot group. The goal is that all the bullet holes should be in close proximity, tightly bunched.

The guy in the command tower, the drill sergeant in this case, seemed to come straight from central casting. Folksy, homey-style, southern drawl. Via loudspeaker, he would give the command to "commence fahrin'," then yell "ceasefahre!" before you walked out into the range to retrieve the target. From the tower, I can still hear the sergeant twanging, "Move out and bring ol' Sarge back a nice, tight shot group." When you returned, if the shot group was too broad, you might get the admonishment: "You've got to have your shit grouped."

As an expression, it may be a little inartful. But it's one way to summarize what you need to do to prepare before an appearance before a large group. Whether it's the friend (you hope) in the audience during one of our town halls or the foe you find in the press or during a corporate board or investor presentation, there will be somebody in your audience who will remind you that it's a good idea to have your message "grouped."

★   ★   ★

Occasionally, my thoughts return to that sales meeting I attended in the early days of my career in leasing. This was the autumn of 1973, the sales conference on Long Island. I still recall how the senior executives from headquarters in San Francisco arrived to talk about sales, customers, market potential, and the overall state of our business. I recall how smoothly and effectively they communicated their message. It was marvelous to watch and hear. Heading back to the office later that week, I wondered not whether I would ever be as accomplished a communicator as these men were but what it would take to get there.

Nearly four decades later, the lesson is clear—confidence in the force of your message, mastery of the message itself, and letting your experience and insight inform style and substance. These are the deciding factors that ultimately determine your ability to connect with your people.

Chapter 15

Charisma Bypass?
Leadership and the
High-Performing Team

During World War II, Katharine Cook Briggs and her daughter, Isabel Briggs Myers, decided they wanted to test a theory—that a working knowledge of personality preferences could help women who were making their first foray into the workforce as part of the war effort. The idea was to learn what kinds of jobs would be the most accessible to women, and what personality styles could be identified that would enable them to achieve the highest levels of productivity.

Obviously, we've moved well beyond the Rosie the Riveter days. As we in senior leadership are acutely aware, the Myers-Briggs test has become a very useful management tool at all levels in the workplace, without doubt the personality assessment most widely employed by American companies. Some estimate that nearly 2 million such tests are administered each year.

Test results are classified by letters that reflect personality styles. For those keeping score, I'm an "INTJ." We who occupy this particular terrain are said to have original minds and an insistence on seeing our ideas and objectives implemented. We are organized and committed to seeing a job through and willing to apply long-range perspectives to our strategic thinking. We're also skeptical and independent, introspective and intuitive, maintaining high standards for ourselves and for our employees. At least that's the conclusion of Myers-Briggs. My profile is shared by about 4 percent of the respondents—mostly CEOs, nuclear physicists, and similar professionals. Or so I've read.

I mention this because there is not anything remotely resembling a one size fits all style of leadership. In fact, quite the opposite is true. While my profile works for me, it may be far different from what defines the chief executives of other companies. All of us in senior management are fully aware of the breadth of leadership styles and preferences.

Leadership roles have been a constant through my personal and professional life. I even ran a squad in the army. I taught kids from Georgia, fresh off the farm without an ounce of sophistication, how to tie their neckties as we readied for the first weekend pass. Yes, it's true. There are a lot of middle-aged men running around the Peach State wearing ties with perfect four-in hand knots, thanks to yours truly. I also helped them write letters home.

I've never been a personality boy, and that's worked just fine for me. There isn't any one style that's better or worse. The best way to get your point across is to be who you are, to be self-aware and able to get your workers to buy into your operating philosophy.

During my years at Compaq and later at Hewlett-Packard Financial Services, I came across strikingly different personalities in the CEO's office. Michael Capellas used to say he was half class clown, half jerk. His successor, Carly Fiorina, had superior platform skills; she was charismatic, but her day-to-day management left something to be desired. Still, she fit the mold of an energetic leader who could deliver a good speech and circulate easily among people, looking for all the world as though she'd just stepped out of a fashion magazine.

Her successor, Mark Hurd, was highly focused and always on task as the CEO of HP. He shunned the spotlight; you'd never see Mark on CNBC dispensing an analysis of the state of the American economy. He always took a pass on the annual global business conference in Davos. He could be tough on his people, maybe excessively so. Where Carly's philosophy was expansive and perhaps unfocused, Mark was much more the bottom-line, nose-to-the-grindstone type of executive.

★　　★　　★

Clearly, lots of leadership styles work. If I had to condense the essence of the successful leader to a few essential managerial qualities, they would be these:

Be true to yourself; people will know if you aren't.
Don't be an asshole. Warren Buffett's "no asshole" rule is one any aspiring leader should adopt.
If you think you're right, and you've done everything you can to support your position, don't deviate.
Never be afraid to lead. People look to their leaders for guidance and inspiration.

Some people just naturally have outgoing personalities. They're great with customers, excel at cocktail party chatter, or exhibit a talent for networking. Funny thing is, while all those personality characteristics are laudable, they don't fit the classic CEO profile. The typical CEO is introverted, capable of envisioning the possibilities but not all that sensitive to the needs and nuances of their colleagues. We can be impersonal, awkward in social settings, but highly disciplined. Maybe those factors are interconnected.

Take a guy like Larry Ellison, the chief executive of Oracle. Larry is a flamboyant character with a flamboyant lifestyle. He loves the headlines and relishes making waves. That's him, and it works just fine for him. Then there's the more traditional style. Leadership Classic. Look at Bob Allen, the former CEO of AT&T who ran the company for a time while we were building AT&T Capital.

People used to call him Mr. Rogers. Was he a success? We were still coming out of the divestiture of the early 1980s, and AT&T was still finding its sea legs, so I'd say the results were mixed. Would a more dynamic figure at the helm during this volatile period have been a better corporate option? It's hard to say.

In moments of repose, all of us who reach this level of leadership ruminate on questions of how style affects our stewardship of the business. How do we best inspire and rally the troops? How do we encourage a committed, energetic response whether it's needed for ups or downs? An effective CEO or other senior leader finds a way to do what it takes: to deliver important messages effectively from the speaker's platform, to have meaningful customer interactions, to present compelling arguments that convince the board of directors of the business value of a particular initiative you hold important.

Outwardly, a leader might appear aloof or even dismissive in certain social situations, but he or she often is just doing what comes naturally. These leaders know what they are about; they don't try to assume a different persona to meet situational demands. They are utterly confident in their ability to do the job.

As for my own leadership style, I'd say my Myers-Briggs assessment is pretty accurate. I can be single-minded and assertive. I'm not going to stop until I realize my objectives. I don't suffer fools gladly. Or at all, usually. But I also think of myself as introspective. The glad-handing, out-among-the-people aspect of the job? Not my favorite part, but I can pull it off when I have to. What I learned from that exceptional U.S. Leasing leadership team at the conference all those years ago in Glen Cove was that charisma and charm can be extremely effective in disseminating your message and galvanizing your team.

If I wind up standing in a corner by myself, I'm not going to be unhappy about it. Put me at a conference table with our executives at corporate headquarters, and I'm in my element. Put me in front of a large crowd, giving a speech about our strategic plan or innovative ideas to raise performance levels, and I feel perfectly at home.

It's not solely about the executive who sits in the big office at the end of the corridor, of course. The executive team you put on the field speaks volumes about you as a business leader. It speaks volumes about your management style and your company's prospects for success. Your people are an extension of you in so many critical ways. I believe that it really boils down to who you want heading into battle with you each and every day. Who do you trust? Who do you want in that foxhole with you? Do your people come to work hungering to perform at the highest possible level?

It's also about how people handle adversity and setbacks once they've reached an elevated position of leadership. Do they make excuses or shift blame? Or do they step up to it and say, "We didn't do our job, we didn't make our number, here's why we didn't make the number, and here's how we'll make it next quarter and for the balance of the year." They have to have that sense of accountability to prosper as a member of my management team.

Throughout my career, I've preached the importance of the self-managed team. That's the basic foundation of my management view—give talented people the opportunity and the tools, share with them a guide map for a successful career, and they will by and large shine. That's how you build the effective, self-managed team. They know what they want to do. They feel empowered.

Making good choices on behalf of the customer, and maintaining operational agility and flexibility, are key facets of any workforce, especially those you entrust with a seat in your inner circle. If you choose wisely in your workplace decisions, infusing them with a tangible sense of strategic and tactical support, you'll keep current customers happy, appeal to potential customers, and, in the end, be successful.

★　　★　　★

Most high-performing teams are capable of rallying around an important task for a designated period. Think of the group at Grumman Corp. They had a specific mission in mind. And when I say mission, I mean it literally. They worked on the rocket that would eventually take astronauts to the moon. It was a 24/7 commitment, fraught with incredible internal and public pressure and tight deadlines, not to mention an entire nation hanging on every development. President Kennedy had proclaimed us destined for the moon by the end of the 1960s, and we were going to the moon, come hell or high water. Is there a more American story of grand public achievement?

I'm no rocket scientist, and companies like ours don't face the same pressurized atmosphere in which those actual, and quite brilliant, rocket scientists and engineers operated. Still, any business with the size and global reach of Hewlett-Packard Financial

Services depends on an integrated senior-level management team to realize its own unique mission. If it's a publicly traded company, as Hewlett-Packard is, there are shareholder demands and considerations that cascade throughout the organization. Failure is not an option.

My definition of a high-performing team—and how it's grown and matured over the years—is one where the players share in an organizing principle, agree on the game plan, and possess enough of the instruments to produce outstanding results quarter after quarter. Sometimes that's not a seamless task. Let's face it, senior management teams are rarely what you'd call completely homogeneous. You're dealing with egos and confidence levels that might be off the charts. They didn't get where they are by being shrinking violets, so they're not going to automatically fall in line and march down the path you've laid out before them.

But it's also a certainty that they do look to the leader for leadership. I firmly believe that even the most self-assured individual wants to be led. They may want to have a full-throated debate over a business direction or process—God knows, we've had more than a few of them during my tenure at HPFS, and Compaq before it—but in the end, the options are usually pretty clear: Get on the train or get left behind.

We do stress open, honest communication among all of our senior managers. We acknowledge the interdependencies and emphasize collaboration. We recognize the need for consistency across the entire organization, from our headquarters in New Jersey to the farthest reaches of South Asia. These are the elements of a high-performing team. You must not only work at the peak level of performance across all these areas; you also have to live the values of your business. As a leader, your every action sets an unmistakable tone for the rest of the company.

To this day, one of my guiding principles is that I surround myself with those who think like I think. Don't mistake that for wanting yes men or yes women. But having people who share my philosophy and management style, and who innately understand how an organization can and should place workers in positions to succeed, is essential.

In evaluating those you're considering hiring, it's very easy to study their track records, review their resumes and educational backgrounds. But you can't look inside their stomachs. You can't have your key teammates stressing or overloading, creating an inappropriate environment from Jump Street. Under stress, we all react in different ways. You have to project, to the best of your ability, exactly how they'll behave in such circumstances.

There's no single marker that ensures the person you hire is going to reach the expected heights. If I'm hiring a direct report, we'll spend a good deal of time together first. But how much of the judgment criteria are based on feeling and how much on the candidate's technical knowledge?

I figure that by the time I sit down with a potential direct report, technical know-how isn't going to be too much of an issue. Experience and demonstrable skill have brought a candidate to the CEO's door. In most cases, candidates already have been through the wars, or else they won't be sitting across from you.

Now it's a question of how they will fit in with the rest of the team: What is their thinking on a broad range of potential decisions and indicators? Are they decisive? In our case, are they willing and prepared to handle the Hewlett-Packard *Stress for Success* environment?

As most successful chief executives must, I have my antennae up. If the intangibles portion of the interview program isn't going quite the way I hoped it would, the hair on the back on my neck tends to start bristling. If the candidate is otherwise a strong potential leader, however, I'll think maybe a second chance is warranted and that I should talk to this person a couple of days down the road. If the hairs start to bristle again on our second meeting, I'll know we need to go in another direction. If you make a mistake, too often it's because you ignore your antennae.

★　　★　　★

In the middle part of the twentieth century, it was said that what was good for General Motors was good for the country. A better corollary might be that what's good for the company is going to be good for all it employs. As a general principle, that's something our managers need to believe. Anybody can be powerful and attempt to lead by dictum. I'm looking for those who can enable others. I want to end up with fewer yes men and women and more who can get things done.

But I do want people who want the same things I want. I've always believed that meeting or exceeding potential is about setting ambitious targets. It's about stretch. You cannot work for me if good enough is *good enough*. We want to be world-class; we insist that you strive to be the top dog in your field. You don't have to step all over others to get there. If you're not willing to stretch yourself and take risks and stick your neck out, you may fall short. You've got to have a noble ambition.

The bottom line is that you have to create the environment and the tone of leadership. You just cannot do otherwise. I guess I'm trying to hire in my own image when I bring someone on board at a senior level. I'd estimate that I've been right 85 to 90 percent of the time in my high-level hires. But, on occasion, you do find yourself in the middle, with a member of your senior team who's dropped the ball but is too valuable to cut loose.

One of our key leaders, with whom I had worked since my days at AT&T, fits that description. We had acquired a company, and I appointed him to run it. It was a plum promotion and one I was convinced that he could handle despite his relatively young age and being untested in a position of this magnitude.

It took him a while to get his operation going. There were signs of struggle out of the gate. One quarter, he missed his plan and missed it by a pretty wide margin. I remember the conversation like it was yesterday, I don't like surprises, and he had given me no heads-up. I said to him that if he ever missed a business plan to that extent again, I'd hang him out to dry. That was my mantra to our top executives: You make your numbers, nobody messes with you. You don't make your numbers, *everybody* messes with you. I'm not a touchy-feely kind of boss.

This particular executive took my tough lesson to heart. He came back the next quarter and made his numbers. The question for me was not "Is he intelligent or able?" My question was, "Does he have the leadership qualities necessary to make it work?" Often, you should take risks because you believe the potential is there. It's just a matter of executing on that potential. And this executive proved to me that he had the right stuff—and the kind of personal drive to turn adversity on its head.

Sometimes, you find yourself a little further out on the limb than where you might be comfortable. More than 20 years ago, I hired a schoolteacher to take a turn as a member of our executive team. She had no experience in business, but I liked what I saw in her. I thought she had the stomach for the job. To me, that's one of those critical intangibles that can make or break a superior leader. Your choice can feel instinctive, but it's instinct built upon experience. That's when you throw the dice.

Some years ago, I had a private tour of the Porsche automobile manufacturing facility in Stuttgart, Germany. Seeing the precision their engineers applied to the manufacture of these incredible cars was something that stays with me to this day. During our tour, we watched one of their engineers build an engine by himself. He wasn't part of an assembly line; he *was* the assembly line.

Once the engine is completed, they submit it to a series of rugged tests, including a heat test of great intensity. And the failure rate is remarkably low, something on the order of 0.04 percent. These engines just don't fail, except on extremely rare occasions. When they do, the engineer isn't chastised, punished, or—worse— terminated. He or she is given additional training. Porsche follows this course of action because the company sincerely believes the engineer isn't just an employee, but an investment.

That's exactly the way to look at it. You invest in a person, and if he performs to expectations most of the time, when that moment of miscalculation arrives or a mistake is made, you roll with it. Help them get back on track, sign them up for a training refresh, maybe change the job focus. Heads shouldn't roll. Because our people have operated under a model all these years that emphasizes ownership of the business, I couldn't do anything less than make sure my colleagues are supported, regardless of the circumstances.

The flip side of the hiring coin is firing. It's never easy. But if you let somebody who must be dealt with just slide, you're failing in your responsibility to all of the others in your organization. In my case, that's 1,500 employees who have put their blood and sweat into making our company the best in the business.

All of our people are looking to me to lead, to make the right choices on their behalf. Hiring or firing employees—from the vice president to the supply room supervisor—is a strategy consideration, a necessary part of risk management, in a way. As chief executive, I'm responsible to the shareholder, to be sure, but I'm also responsible to my workers. The tone at the top is critical to success or failure.

There have been a few missteps along the way. I haven't always been dead on in my hiring—if, as I surmise, I've been right in making top-level choices in management personnel 85 to 90 percent of the time, that leaves the other 10 to 15 percent. In the early days of my tenure as the CEO of Compaq, I hired a sales manager after searching for nearly a year. The candidate was very impressive throughout the hiring process. He was smart and dynamic, seemingly a natural fit—and he turned out to be a disaster—impulsive and tending to go his own way. I fired him 30 days later. I was fast on the trigger, but I realized very quickly it wasn't going to work. It was an example of not going along to get along.

In the case of one of my regional managers in our Asia Pacific region, the sacking was a longer time in the making. I had hopped a plane and flown halfway around the world to tell him we were letting him go—he was based in Australia. I probably could have told him over the phone, but I really wanted to tell him in person. Once I arrived at our regional headquarters, we sat there in the office waiting for him to show up. He never did. So I fired him over the phone after all, jumped back on the plane, and home I went.

On many occasions, you're taking on a senior leader who is supported by your bosses. That can be a delicate situation, and I found myself in one with the managing director of HP Tech Finance European and Middle East region after the Compaq/HP merger was finalized in 2002. From a practical and political standpoint, I didn't want to supplant the entire HP customer financing team immediately with my own people. The MD of that region was a holdover, a rising star within HP, a Stanford graduate and experienced in the industry.

But we never clicked. Despite his popularity along the C-suite at HP headquarters, after 12 months I came to understand that we needed to part ways. Our business philosophies were at odds; I wasn't happy with the way he was managing his operation. His performance left much to be desired; he wasn't hitting the numbers he had committed to; he was an ineffective leader.

I flew to Geneva in early 2004 to fire him. I told him he wasn't getting it done, that we needed a change. I was accompanied by a Human Resources representative to walk him through the severance package. The whole meeting took about 10 minutes. It was a very unpleasant experience; the executive was angry that he was being let go after 18 years with the company. But by that point, I didn't really care.

Managing a multibillion-dollar enterprise can never be a popularity contest. You can't be afraid to take on a board of directors, or the CEO of a parent organization who oversees your operation, even if the firing decision affects one of their favorite sons (or daughters).

It's not always strictly a question of performance and skill that leads to a decision to cut ties. A key measurement of the senior leadership team goes beyond core competence. Those around you need to be trustworthy, to embrace and execute the strategy even if, personally, they might prefer another route.

We continually talk to our managers about this. We provide specific and pointed training. There is a zero tolerance policy. We just can't have people doing their own thing. We have to preserve a sound control environment. Any leader should welcome creative thinking on the part of his key players, even a little dissonance if it might improve customer relations and the bottom line, but wholesale disregard for the commitments we make, especially to each other, is unacceptable.

For me, the senior management team I've assembled over the years encompasses all the attributes of the successful leader. It's an ambitious group. They want to perform at the highest levels and are determined to move us forward. They all take their cue from me, which I concede can be a challenge at times. I never do the Happy Dance; that's what my team calls it, the idea that we can take our eye off the ball for more than a few minutes to bask in the glow of success, celebrate, and enjoy what we've accomplished. We're always working at higher tasks, striving for bigger, better, and stronger. Despite the joking entreaties of my managers, I've never done the Happy Dance. And you shouldn't expect it any time soon.

Leadership style is distilled from many experiences and sources. Your sources of inspiration and knowledge can come from anywhere, whether it's a valued number two in the C-suite, business colleagues, family member, or a best friend. My oldest and dearest friend is Alan Ulan. We've been friends for 40 years, since our early twenties. I was fresh out of the army when we met; he was fresh out of college. Alan is a stockbroker in New York City. We speak on the phone nearly every day, even if it's only for 30 seconds. We have an ongoing dispute over who is the best dresser in America. He thinks he is, I think I am, naturally. He's also fond of telling me how good he looks. He'll call me up, "How're you doing, pussycat?"

"I'm doing fine, sweetie pie," I'll say. It's as if we're a couple of old Jewish grandfathers, *kvetching,* yelling at each other, ashes from burning cigars falling on our sweater vests. We take on these personas. In some ways, we're as different as can be. Alan doesn't have a cell phone. He thinks an iPad is something you slip under a mattress. I run the financing business of a global computer company. Not only do I have a BlackBerry, it's never turned off.

The value in having a long-time trusted friend such as Alan is that he keeps me grounded. I have a special executive team— some of them have been with me nearly three decades, such as Gerri Gold and Dan McCarthy. Their contributions to our corporate success are incalculable. But preserving that bond with a best friend brings a welcome outside perspective to my thinking. Even if we're only fighting over who wears the best suits, it's special, even unique.

Alan and I have a pact: Whoever dies first, the survivor gets the ties of the dead guy. But it's more than that. The survivor must look inside the casket and make sure the dimple is in the middle of the tie being worn by the deceased. If not, you have to reach in and fix it. It's a blood oath. With great ties comes great responsibility.

★ ★ ★

Early in my career, I wondered how the road to success would unwind. It hasn't always been the way I thought it would be. Sometimes the road signs point you in directions you might not expect. Taking that Wall Street job in the mid-1980s was one of those decisions that was life-changing in ways I never anticipated at the time.

One facet of my leadership philosophy that hasn't changed a bit over the years is that I'm never satisfied, regardless of objectives achieved and results posted. The roughest time for me profession-ally is actually achieving, or even exceeding, my goals. When that happens, I almost immediately go through a couple of months of struggle. I have to know, almost from the start, what the next objective is and how I can attain it. Once I've got that figured out, everything will be fine because I believe I can set the right course. But I feel burdened by a nagging sense of unease in the meantime.

It's like the football coach who, the morning after his victori-ous Super Bowl, is back in the training room. He's watching game film, searching for advantages over his opponents. He's reviewing the list of potential free agents and draft choices. He refuses to rest on his laurels, even for one day, even in the afterglow of a seismic personal accomplishment.

I imagine Tom Coughlin, the coach of my beloved New York Giants, going right back at it while his upset of the New England Patriots in the big game in 2007 (and again this year) was still fresh in his mind. That sounds like me—you win the Super Bowl, have a couple of glasses of champagne, and get back to the drawing board. In hockey, the winners carry the Stanley Cup around for three months, and then it's on to the next season. I have to confess, that kind of prolonged celebration mystifies me.

The analogy of the hard-driving CEO to the successful football coach is instructive, I think. We depend on our analytical skills, we demand as much data as possible, and then we factor in our own instincts and perspective. Are you willing to be held accountable? Are you smart enough to turn around a bad situation? Do your people feel like they want to run through the wall for you?

The cloak of successful leadership isn't cut from a single cloth. The leadership qualities I've developed over the years work for me. At the end of the day, you've got to be able to look in the mirror and ask yourself: "Have I done everything I can to promote a strategy that's in the best interests of our workforce, our customers, and our positioning in the industry?"

If the answer is yes, you've got a leadership style that's working.

Chapter 16

To There, From Here

A wise man once observed that "the future is just one damned thing after another." No crystal ball sits at the corner of your desk to illuminate your thinking and crystallize where your career may be heading. There will be no shortage of challenges coming the way of every chief executive as we work deeper into the twenty-first century.

Predicting the future can be a fool's errand; enacting a strategy to keep unpleasant future surprises to a minimum belongs to the CEO. Ronald Reagan, as he was on so many occasions, was right about this—stay the course. Find a plan that works for you and that you understand almost intuitively will work. When the gale winds of doubt begin to howl, hold steady.

It may sound like I'm stealing a page from the Boy Scout Handbook, but staying true to yourself (and never deviating from your fundamental vision) is a prescription for career success. It's not always the case, but most of the time, I'm convinced, true talent and vision rises to the top.

Bob Kavner was the chief financial officer of AT&T at the time I was serving as CFO of AT&T Capital Corp. I had great respect for him, and we maintained a dotted line relationship. He used to say to me, "Irv, you know what your problem is? You're about two inches wide and three miles deep. We've got to change that."

I never really understood why. I would always respond, "Well, what's wrong with that? I'm doing what I've got to do. And what's more, I'm doing it well. You can try and change me, but to what end?"

I've never looked at my career path, at those things that appealed most to me in terms of advancement, as excuses for overly aggressive competitive behavior. Politics was never my strength or my affinity, as my battles at AT&T Capital, the board at Compaq and other senior leaders along the way attest. It wouldn't be the kind of thing I would dwell on, to be honest. People are always trying to push their own agendas, or so it seems. My team has been with me a long time, and they know I have no patience for that.

In the final analysis, to my way of thinking, the recipe for leadership success isn't overly complicated. Hard work is a given. Passion for what you do and sticking to your principles, these too are essential. Innovation, creative business planning, a singular vision? These are the ingredients that ultimately may separate the good corporate executive from the greats.

All of those attributes of leadership will be in greater demand as we, as a business community, push deeper into the murky waters of a rapidly changing, and never-so-challenging, global economic world. The Great Recession changed the landscape, perhaps forever. The Industry Future Council, the group of my peers that assesses the state of the leasing and finance union, called it "the Great Reset," and I think that's an apt description of the dangers we were forced to confront then and still must navigate. Mother Nature contributed her share of extraordinary if not tragic events in 2011: the tsunami in Japan leading to a potential nuclear disaster, flooding in Thailand are two that come to mind. You can theorize that these were unprecedented events and therefore impossible to prepare for. I disagree. Unprecedented events always happen, but if you take the time to do a worst-case scenario, update it periodically and construct a detailed recovery trajectory that can be implemented quickly, you position yourself and your company for the best possible recovery result. "What do we do now?" is too late.

Our margin for error is much smaller now than it was even as recently as 2006. At this writing, the economy continues its crawl toward what we all consider normal. The successful executive of the future must adapt, remain open to innovation and change, and yet retain and apply his or her core principles. Nobody said that's an easy tightrope to walk. Certainly, it wasn't for me as I moved from the intense sales environment of Wall Street to high-pressure leadership roles at three successive multibillion-dollar captive finance companies.

No chief executive will escape the corporate gauntlet without at least a few scars. At least none I know ever has. But, as your career works its way through the back nine, if you've remained true to your vision and let your experience and instinct be your guides, perhaps you can be forgiven for looking backward and thinking, "Not bad. Not bad at all."

About the Author

Irv Rothman is President and CEO of HP Financial Services, a wholly owned subsidiary of Hewlett-Packard Company.

Irv is responsible for the worldwide delivery of customized leasing, financing and financial asset management solutions that simplify customers' IT lifecycle management and reduce their total cost of ownership. HP Financial Services supports all customer needs, from the largest corporate accounts to small and mid-sized businesses.

The company is headquartered in Berkeley Heights, New Jersey, with regional headquarters in Dublin, Ireland, and Sydney, Australia. HP Financial Services has 1,500 employees worldwide and does business in more than 50 countries. It is the second-largest captive IT leasing company in the world.

Prior to joining HP, Irv was President and CEO of Compaq Financial Services Corporation (CFS). He led CFS from its founding in 1997, growing the business to greater than $3.7 billion in total assets prior to the HP-Compaq merger.

With over 38 years in the leasing industry, Irv held leadership positions with U.S. Leasing International and Thomson McKinnon Securities before joining AT&T in 1985. As a group president of AT&T Capital Corporation, he helped build an organization that ultimately grew to be the second largest leasing company in the country.

Irv attended Rutgers University and earned an MBA from Pepperdine University. He and his wife, Franziska, live in Chatham, NJ and Nokomis, FL.

Index

Index

Index

Index

Index

Index

Index

Networking, 63
New York Times, 56–57, 75, 181

One company worldwide
  philosophy, 103
Operating model, 9, 72, 95, 181.
  See also Business model
Operations, day-to-day
  accountability, 154
  achievement vs. plan, 156
  Brazil, 159
  in business plan, 155, 157
  business plan is inviolate
    (expression), 155
  calendared meetings with
    direct reports, 154
  chaebols, 157
  check-in meetings, 154
  custom sales, 160
  with a customer, 160
  customer interaction, 157
  customer satisfaction, 154
  customer service, 158
  Dan McCarthy on Rothman,
    154
  day-to-day operations, 154
  delegation of, 153
  with direct reports, 154
  dirty-fingernails, 154, 160
  General Motors Brazil, 159
  growing the business, 156
  Japan, 157
  keiretsu, 157
  knowledge of business model,
    154

  leadership team performance,
    154
  long-range plans, 156
  micromanaging, 155
  performance of, 154
  quorums, 155
  South Korea, 157–158
  stretch in business plan, 155, 157
  trading houses, 157
  value proposition, 160
Organization choices, 7–8
Organization Planning and
  Design, Inc., 6
Organization reporting, 60
Out-executing the competition,
  77
Overhead exposure and expenses,
  116
Ownership sense, 10

Partnerships, 109–110
Passion, 200
Pepperdine University, 48, 49, 51.
  See also College experiences
Personal relationships, 63
Peru, 109
Pfeiffer, Eckhard
  acquisition mode, 131
  COMPAQ departure, 121, 135
  executive team, 106
  Rothman meeting with, 86–87
  speed of growth, 93, 109–110
Phil, 44–45
Planning and implementation,
  169

Index